POPULAR PROGRAMS
BASED ON
HYMN STORIES

POPULAR PROGRAMS
Based on Hymn Stories

ERNEST K. EMURIAN

BAKER BOOK HOUSE · Grand Rapids, Michigan

Reprinted, May, 1972, by
Baker Book House Company

ISBN: 0-8010-3269-5

Formerly printed under the title
Hymn Festivals

Printed in the United States of America

To
those Church Officers
who
through the years of my pastorates
have
by their loving loyalty
enriched my life and ministry
and
permitted me to engage in many activities
which have resulted in my own personal development
and in the growth and strengthening
of our church.

PREFACE

This book was prepared at the insistent suggestion of many ministers and laymen before whom the writer has lectured and for whom he has presented these *Popular Programs Based on Hymn Stories*. These programs have met with an enthusiastic response in such places as Constitution Hall, Washington, D. C. where several of these programs were presented by the author, who directed the mammoth Hymn Sing sponsored by several hundred Methodist congregations there for two consecutive years; the summer assemblies at the Methodist Conference ground at Lake Junaluska, North Carolina; as well as at many different summer schools for ministers at Emory University, Georgia, and several Methodist Annual Conference sessions and pastor's conferences and schools scattered throughout America. Participants and worshipers in many of these gatherings felt that a volume of this nature would fill a need for leaders who are on the constant lookout for unusual, practical, inspiration programs for Sunday evening services, mid-week services, and other meetings of this sort. Consequently, these programs may be readily adapted to local situations by deletions or additions, and by substituting solos, duets, quartets or choral selections in many instances, according to talent available.

Most of the hymns and gospel songs included in this collection may be found in the standard hymnals and songbooks of nearly every denomination. In the event some are difficult to find, let the stanzas be mimeographed for distribution or printed in the bulletin for congregational participation. Supplementary material about many authors and composers may be found in any of the published books by the writer, all publications of Baker Book House and listed on the frontispiece of this volume. They contain a wealth of information regarding the origin of many hymns, gospel songs and hymn tunes, background material not found in any other collection of this type.

The author is grateful to all whose valuable assistance made this book a reality, and he offers this publication to the interested public with the hope that these programs may result in a deeper appreciation of the lives of the heroes and heroines of every hymnal and a more intelligent evaluation of the spiritual experiences out of which many of our noblest hymns and finest gospel songs were born.

Ernest K. Emurian
Cherrydale Methodist Church
Arlington, Virginia

CONTENTS

Hymns of All Churches   13

Heroes of The Hymnal   23

Heroines of The Hymnal   35

Isaac Watts: Singing A New Song   43

Charles Wesley: Praise Ye The Lord   53

John Newton: Growing In Grace   65

Reginald Heber: The Church Year   75

Samuel Francis Smith: Christian Patriotism   87

Fanny Crosby: Blessed Assurance   97

A Missionary Hymn Festival   109

Miscellaneous Programs: 119

    An Alphabetical Hymn Festival   119

    A Chronological Hymn Festival:
    hymns of all ages   121

    A Biblical Hymn Festival   123

    A Geographical Hymn Festival:
    hymns of all nations   124

HYMNS OF ALL CHURCHES

HYMNS OF ALL CHURCHES

Baptist: America; Blest Be The Tie That Binds; He leadeth Me

Presbyterian: This Is My Father's World; O Love That Wilt Not Let Me Go; Rock Of Ages (Ivory Palaces)

Episcopalian (Anglican): The Doxology; Abide With Me; O Little Town of Bethlehem (The Star Spangled Banner)

Unitarian: Nearer My God To Thee (Holy Spirit, Truth Divine)

Quaker: Dear Lord And Father Of Mankind

Roman Catholic: Shepherd Of Tender Youth; Faith Of Our Fathers

Jewish: The Lord's My Shepherd, I'll Not Want

Lutheran: A Mighty Fortress Is Our God

Brethren: What A Friend We Have In Jesus

Congregational-Christian: The Way Of The Cross Leads Home; Beautiful Isle Of Somewhere; O Master Let Me Walk With Thee; My Faith Looks Up To Thee

Salvation Army: The Old Rugged Cross

Methodist: Love Divine; Jesus, Lover Of My Soul; Blessed Assurance

The great hymns and spiritual songs of our faith have become the common property of all branches of Christendom, because they emphasize those beliefs and experiences which every denomination shares with every other denomination. Those who sing these sacred hymns and songs often have no idea from what branch of the Church they have come, nor are they particularly interested or concerned. They rejoice that in every different division of the Church there are those whom God has inspired to sing of those truths which are the proud possessions of all of God's children, of every clime and of every time. Thus the Salvation Army worker can sing with the Presbyterian a Roman Catholic hymn "Faith Of Our Fathers", just as the devout Catholic can blend his voice with the Baptist in singing the Unitarian hymn "Nearer My God To Thee". If every sacred song except those of a particular denomination were removed from the hymnals and song-books of each denomination, congregational singing would gradually disappear from the Churches of Christendom.

In fact, while some Christians hesitate to recite a creed with other believers, they will sing their convictions together in a hymn of praise without realizing that they are more united in singing than in speaking. Possibly it was for that reason that God gave us the gift of song. As we sing the hymns and songs of twelve different religious organizations or denominations, let us rejoice that we have such a God and can jointly praise Him as we lift our hearts as well as our voices together and present unto him our songs as one of our "sacrifices of thanksgiving".

BAPTIST

The greatest patriotic hymn in American history came from the pen of a twenty-three year old student for the Baptist ministry, Rev. Samuel Francis Smith, in the year 1832, while he was pursuing his theological studies at the Theological Seminary in Andover, Massachusetts, and it is our beloved unofficial national anthem, "America". No nobler statement of Christian convictions and patriotic sentiments has come from any American pen, and it is significant that a Protestant clergyman gave poetic utterance to these feelings in the four stanzas of this majestic hymn. Let us sing together the first and fourth stanzas of "My Country, 'Tis Of Thee".

The most popular hymn of Christian fellowship in all hymnody also came from the pen of a Baptist divine, the British Baptist minister, Rev. John Fawcett, who penned his beautiful hymn, "Blest Be The Tie That Binds", in the study of his Church in Wainsgate, England, shortly after declining a call to serve the large and influential Carter's Lane Baptist Church in London. Turning down that flattering invitation, he remained at his humble post for forty-five more years, dying in Wainsgate July 25, 1817 at the age of seventy-seven. Let us sing together the first two stanzas of this well-known and familiar hymn.

— — — — — — — —

It was a twenty-eight year old Baptist minister, Rev. Joseph Henry Gilmore (1834-1918), who versified the Twenty-third Psalm into the gospel hymn "He Leadeth Me, O Blessed Thought", writing his stanzas in March, 1862, shortly after speaking on that Psalm to a mid-week congregation in Philadelphia's First Baptist Church, during the darkest days of the tragic Civil War. Set to music shortly thereafter by the prolific composer of sacred songs, William Bradbury, this is as fine a hymn as this beloved Psalm has ever inspired. Let us sing together "He Leadeth Me".

PRESBYTERIAN

One of the most popular hymns by a Presbyterian clergyman is "This Is My Father's World", which Rev. Maltbie Davenport Babcock wrote, possibly during his first pastorate at the Presbyterian Church in Lockport, New York. Following his brief stay there, he accepted the call to serve a large Presbyterian congregation in Baltimore, going from there to succeed Dr. Henry Van Dyke at New York City's famous Brick Presbyterian Church. Another well known hymn from his pen is entitled "Be Strong!". He passed away suddenly and tragically at the age of forty-three, while returning from a Palestinian trip on which he had gone as much in search of renewed health as well as to visit the sites and scenes associated with Our Lord's earthly ministry. Let us sing together one stanza of this familiar hymn, which appeared in print in a volume published by his widow the year after the minister's death in 1901.

—— —— —— —— ——

The Rev. George Matheson, (1842-1906) the brilliant blind Scottish preacher, author and poet, wrote his finest hymn during his fortieth year, in 1882, while serving the Presbyterian congregation at Innellan, Argylshire, Scotland. While he wrote many books on a wide variety of subjects and was recognized as one of the most influential ministers of his day, this one hymn alone has immortalized his name among Christians the world over, for it is the well-known devotional poem, "O Love That Wilt Not Let Me Go". Let us sing the first stanza together.

—— —— —— —— ——

Of course, "Rock Of Ages" is about as Calvinistic a hymn as there is, coming from the prolific and sometimes caustic pen of the militant minister and editor Augustus Montague Toplady (1740-1778) who wrote his words, according to tradition, in 1776 on the back of a playing card, the six of diamonds, while hiding in a cleft of a great rock in Burrington Gorge in a remote rural section of his native England. While Toplady had little patience with the Arminian theology of the Wesleys, strangely enough his hymn and Charles Wesley's "Jesus, Lover Of My Soul" are among the world's favorites today. Let us sing together "Rock Of Ages".

—— —— —— —— ——

(Here the gospel song "Ivory Palaces" which the Presbyterian pianist Henry Barraclough wrote at the Presbyterian Assembly ground at Montreat, North Carolina in the summer of 1915, following a sermon on Psalm 45:8 by the well-known evangelist Dr. J. Wilbur Chapman, may be sung as a solo or duet.)

EPISCOPAL (ANGLICAN)

The most popular Anglican hymn is a four-line Long Meter poem with which the English poet Bishop Thomas Ken (1637-1711) concluded many of his lengthy paeans of praise, the bit of poetry we speak of as "The Doxology". As we sing this response together, let us remember that it was first a part of a hymn, and represents Episcopalian hymn-writing at its best.

— —— —— —— —— ——

The British Anglican minister, Rev. Henry Francis Lyte, (1793-1847) was the author of such well-known hymns as "Praise My Soul The King Of Heaven" and "Jesus, I My Cross Have Taken", but his best hymn, which was completed shortly before his death from tuberculosis, was dated September 4, 1847, and is known by the first three words of the opening stanza, "Abide With Me". Within six weeks after putting the final touches on this, his "swan-song", Lyte was dead. Let us sing now one stanza of this noble hymn of faith and affirmation in the face of sorrow and death.

— —— —— —— —— ——

It was an American Episcopalian, Rev. Phillips Brooks (1835-1893), who wrote one of Christendom's loveliest Christmas carols, "O Little Town Of Bethlehem". The thirty-three year old bachelor penned his stanzas in 1868, three years after a memorable visit to the Holy Land, as he reminisced over his experiences and prepared a program for the children of his Church, the Holy Trinity Church, Philadelphia. Set to music by his close friend and Church organist, another bachelor, Lewis Redner, this carol grows increasingly popular with the passing of the years. The tune was named "St. Louis" by the poet-preacher, who wished to honor his organist without embarrassing him, hence the changing of the spelling of the composer's first name. Let us sing one stanza of this popular carol.

— —— —— —— —— ——

(An Episcopalian layman, the American lawyer Francis Scott Key, wrote the official national anthem of the United States, "The Star Spangled Banner", in September, 1814, which may also be sung if time permits. Any hymn by Anglican Bishop Reginald Heber, Rev. Isaac Watts, Rev. Sabine Baring-Gould or Miss Frances Ridley Havergal can be used here. Information about them and about their hymns may be found in other chapters in this collection.)

17

UNITARIAN

President William McKinley's favorite hymn came from the pen of an English Unitarian, Mrs. Sarah Flower Adams (1805-1848), who wrote her one famous hymn, "Nearer My God To Thee", at the request of her minister, Rev. William J. Fox, who served the South Place Religious Society, Finsbury, England, in which congregation the talented woman held her membership. Inspired by the Old Testament account of Jacob's dream, Genesis 28: 10-22, Mrs. Adams completed her best-known hymn just eight years prior to her untimely death from tuberculosis in 1848 at the age of forty-three. Set to music by the Father of American Hymnology, Dr. Lowell Mason, this hymn is one of the few Unitarian hymns to be found in the hymnals of trinitarian congregations.

(Another Unitarian hymn came from the pen of an American Unitarian minister, Rev. Samuel Longfellow (1819-1892) one of whose finest hymns is "Holy Spirit, Truth Divine".) Let us sing together one stanza of "Nearer My God To Thee".

QUAKER

The Quaker poet, John Greenleaf Whittier (1807-1892) rebelled against the emotional excesses of early New England revivals, and wrote "The Brewing Of Soma" as his poetic protest against what he considered violently unChristian practices. From these stirring stanzas the hymn "Dear Lord And Father Of Mankind" is taken. Let us sing one stanza of this hymn from the pen of this spiritual son of George Fox, the founder of the Quaker witness, and the proclaimer of "the inner light".

ROMAN CATHOLIC

Any Christian hymn that antedates The Protestant Reformation can claim Catholic authorship, and the translations by Rev. John Neale of the hymns of the ancient saints, or other translations of the hymns of the Bernards (of Clairvaux and Cluny) are also truly Catholic. However, the earliest Christian hymn in existence is Henry Dexter's 1846 poetic rendition of Bishop Clement of Alexandria's second-century free-verse poem, which is our hymn "Shepherd Of Tender Youth". Sung to the tune "Italian Hymn-Trinity" (Come Thou Almighty King) this is still a splendid hymn for adults as well as young people. Let us sing together the first stanza of this ancient hymn to this familiar tune.

———————

The British Catholic Priest, Rev. Frederick Faber (1814-1863), wanted to do for his Church what Watts and Wesley did for theirs, so he wrote many fine hymns, among them one that contained this statement, "Faith Of Our Fathers, Mary's Prayers, Shall Win All England Unto Thee". As Protestantized by subsequent authors and editors, this poem from the pen of a talented Roman priest is our thrilling hymn, "Faith Of Our Fathers". Let us sing one stanza together, as we recall our Catholic heritage.

JEWISH

While Jewish people do not sing Christian hymns, Christian people continue to sing Jewish hymns, for any sacred poem based upon or inspired by one of the Old Testament Psalms is actually a Jewish hymn. One of the most majestic of our Judeo-Christian hymns is British newspaper editor Joseph Addison's poem "The Spacious Firmament On High" based upon Psalm Nineteen. But a more familiar one is "The Lord's My Shepherd, I'll Not Want", inspired by Psalm Twenty-three. Let us sing this hymn together, remembering that in so doing we are acknowledging our Jewish heritage as well as affirming our Christian hope.

LUTHERAN

From the prolific and powerful pen of Martin Luther himself, who was the spiritual father of the Protestant Reformation, came the mighty strains of the militant battlesong, "A Mighty Fortress Is Our God". It was in the summer of 1529 that the forty-five year old ex-priest poeticized his convictions in the stanzas that have lived to this very day.

Let us sing now the first stanza of Luther's hymn to the tune which he himself composed for his own lines. Since the hymn is a unit, we will read together the remaining stanzas after we have sung the first.

BRETHREN

There are many branches of The Brethren Church, so for all of them we will sing the hymn of the transplanted Irish Brethren lay-preacher, Joseph Scriven (1819-1886) who wrote this hymn at Bewdley overlooking Rice Lake, about ten miles north of Port Hope, Ontario, in Canada about 1855. Set to music by C. C. Converse some years later, it was first printed as the last hymn in a Richmond, Virginia publication. The editors lived to confess that "the last hymn in the book became the first in the hearts of the people". Scriven's hymn is, of course, "What A Friend We Have In Jesus". Let us sing it together now.

CHRISTIAN

The best-known poet of the Christian Church (and there are several different branches of Christendom that use this name, including those known as The Disciples) was the wife of a prominent Indianapolis minister, Mrs. Jesse Brown Pounds (1861-1921). From her pen came the stanzas of two popular gospel songs "The Way Of The Cross Leads Home" set to music by composer Charles H. Gabriel, and her sentimental song about heaven, "Beautiful Isle Of Somewhere" which she wrote in 1896 when her husband was serving the Central Christian Church in the Indiana city. Composer John Sylvester Fearis (1867-1932), whose popular ditty "Little Sir Echo" is still being sung by children the country over, set Mrs. Pound's words to music in 1897, and they are still being sung throughout the English-singing world as one author's poetic description of the world to come. (Here a soloist may sing "Beautiful Isle Of Somewhere" after which the congregation may sing one stanza of "The Way Of The Cross Leads Home".)

CONGREGATIONAL

While this great Church has recently united with several branches of The Christian Church, she can look with pride to the fact that her denomination has produced more virile hymns of the Christian social awakening than any other branch of divided Christendom. A Congregational clergyman who was a "great leader for civic righteousness", Dr. Washington Gladden (1836-1918), wrote his famous hymn "O Master, Let Me Walk With Thee" in 1879. The tune to which we sing his stanzas, "Maryton", was originally composed for Rev. John Keble's hymn "Sun Of My Soul". Let us sing the first stanza of this hymn together.

————————

One of our finest hymns of personal devotion, "My Faith Looks Up To Thee", also came from the pen of a Congregational clergyman, Rev. Ray Palmer (1808-1887), who wrote his moving stanzas when he was just twenty-one years of age, and prior to his entering the active ministry. Two years later Dr. Lowell Mason coaxed the words out of the poet and set them to music, naming his tune "Olivet", and prophesying that years after the minister was dead, he would be remembered principally because of those four beautiful stanzas, a prophecy which time has proved to be true. Let us sing now two stanzas of "My Faith Looks Up To Thee". (The Church Dr. Palmer served in Albany, New York was moved recently from its original downtown location to a suburban area, and renamed The Ray Palmer Memorial Congregational Church.)

SALVATION ARMY

The Rev. George Bennard was connected with The Salvation Army when he went to Pokagon, Michigan in the early summer of 1913 to conduct a series of revival services in the Methodist Church. During that memorable week, many experiences converged to inspire him to write the words and music of what was to become the most popular gospel song in all the world, "The Old Rugged Cross". The success of this sacred song goes to prove that age cannot make a bad song good or a good song bad, and also that a good song is readily accepted by the people and taken to their hearts, so suddenly sometimes that they actually believe their favorite is an "old, old song" which grandmother used to sing. If she did, she had to live after 1913, for this popular song is not yet ready to celebrate its Golden Anniversary. Let us sing now "The Old Rugged Cross".

METHODIST

From the pen of the co-founder of Methodism, Rev. Charles Wesley (1807-1888) came six-thousand of the greatest hymns in the world, among them "Love Divine", "Hark, The Herald Angels Sing", and "Jesus, Lover Of My Soul". (Sing one stanza of one or two of these hymns here.) Also from the pen of a Methodist, this time an American woman, blind Fanny Crosby (1820-1915), came some of the finest gospel songs in all sacred literature, among her finest hymns being "Blessed Assurance", "Safe In The Arms Of Jesus", "Saved By Grace" and "I Am Thine, O Lord". Let us conclude our HYMNS OF ALL CHURCHES by singing one stanza of Wesley's "Love Divine" and one of Fanny Crosby's "Blessed Assurance". (The stories of these hymns are included in other chapters in this volume.)

HEROES OF THE HYMNAL

Rev. Sabine Baring-Gould; Poet and Composer:
        Onward Christian Soldiers
        Now The Day Is Over (Tune: Eudoxia)
William B. Bradbury; Composer:
        On Christ The Solid Rock I Stand
        He Leadeth Me
        Sweet Hour Of Prayer
        Saviour Like A Shepherd Lead Us
        Jesus Loves Me
        Tis Midnight And On Olive's Brow
        Just As I Am Without One Plea
Rev. Henry Francis Lyte; Poet:
        Praise My Soul The King Of Heaven
        Jesus I My Cross Have Taken
        Abide With Me
Rev. Robert Lowry; Poet and Composer:
        We're Marching To Zion
        I Need Thee Every Hour
        Shall We Gather At The River
        All The Way My Saviour Leads Me
        Something For Thee
        Christ Arose!

Any Hymnal or Songbook is the result of the lives, loves and labors of many men and women over the span of many centuries from many different lands and countries. Most of them are one-hymn poets or one-tune composers, their sole legacy consisting in the single hymn or the single tune they were privileged to bequeath to subsequent generations. However, there occasionally appeared on the hymnic scene a musician who also proved himself a successful poet or a poet who was a musician and composer as well, and Christendom accepted both their poems and their tunes as worthy instruments for the praise of God. There were also such poets as Watts, Wesley and Heber who have many of their finest hymns in the collections of nearly all denominations, while such musicians as Sullivan, Mason, Dykes and Bradbury have many tunes in the hymnals of the universal Church. This particular Hymn Festival, Heroes of the Hymnal, will feature the poems of two remarkable English divines, and the tunes and stanzas of two American composers. As we sing these hymns and gospel songs, let us rejoice that God has seen fit to reveal Himself through many different kinds of poetry and many different types of music, by means of which He can still draw men unto Himself and build them up in the most holy faith.

———————————

One of the most remarkable men in the history of English hymnody was the Rev. Sabine Baring-Gould, who was at the same time an effective clergyman of the Church of England, a very prolific author and novelist, who, prior to his death at the age of ninety in 1924 had written and published more books than any other Englishman up to that time, and a hymn-writer who left as one of his finest legacies two hymns that are about as different in content and mood as day and night: the evening prayer "Now The Day Is Over" and the militant stanzas of "Onward Christian Soldiers". Baring-Gould was serving his first parish at Horbury Bridge in Yorkshire, England, when he fell desperately in love with Grace Taylor, the daughter of a mill-hand in his own congregation. He sent Grace away to school to have her educated, and then married her, performing the ceremony himself, one of the few ministers who had nerve enough to "blame himself" for his own wedding! It was when he was preparing for a WhitMonday outing for the boys and girls of his Horbury Bridge parish in the late spring of 1864, his fortieth year, that he searched in vain for a good marching song which the children could sing as they walked down the little country lanes to meet another group at a picnic spot about seven miles away. When he found nothing to his liking, he dashed off a few original stanzas of his own, picked up a theme from Haydn's "Symphony in D" as an appropriate tune, and taught his little charges to sing "Onward Christian Soldiers". He didn't know it at the time, but he had just put the finishing touches on the most militant hymn that British Christendom was to give to world Christianity. Remember as we sing this hymn together, not to the poet's musical arrangement but to the stirring strains that Sir Arthur Sullivan composed for Baring-Gould's stanzas in 1871, that it was written for a children's outing, and although it is militant in spirit, there was no thought of penning a militaristic song for adult soldiers in the preacher-poet's mind when he wrote his lines for his juniors and intermediates. Let us sing together "Onward Christian Soldiers".

— — — — — — — — —

Baring-Gould inherited his father's estate, Lew Trenchard, and moved there in 1872, spending the remainder of his long and active life there on the three-thousand acres of this ancestral estate. More than eighty books on a wide variety of subjects came from his prolific pen including reminiscences, novels, biographical sketches, histories and miscellaneous writings of a sacred and secular nature. But it was in 1865, the year after he wrote his militant hymn, that he wrote what he called "An Evening Hymn for Missions", which is now our beautiful Sunday evening hymn, "Now The Day Is Over". Again he arranged original music for his lines, this time harmonizing a simple little tune he had heard in Germany when, during his post-graduate years, he had taken a leisurely trip through several European countries. This tune, "Eudoxia", may be found in several hymnals today, but it has long since been supplanted by Joseph Barnby's lovely tune "Merrial". Against this interesting background, let us sing together "Now The Day Is Over", remembering that these two hymns constantly remind us that as Christians we are to be both militant and meditative.

— — — — — — — — —

A different kind of hymnological hero was the New England composer William Batchelder Bradbury, whose life of fifty-two years began in 1816 and ended in 1868, but who, in that span of years, edited, published and assisted in the publication of more books, volumes and collections of music than the years of his earthly pilgrimage. It was Dr. Lowell Mason who saw the genius in Bradbury and brought him to Boston both to work and to study in the field of sacred music. The young man's first position, however, lasted just about twenty-minutes, for, when he sat down at the console of the organ of a Boston Church in the presence of the assembled music committee members, he discovered that the instrument was so old-fashioned that an assistant was needed not only to pump up the bellows but also to pull up some of the lower keys. The committee promised him $25 a year if he accepted the position as organist, but when the musician insisted that he needed an additional $25 for pulling up the keys as well as pushing them down, they quickly terminated his tenure as Church organist. After serving another Church in Machias, Maine, and trying his hand at various other church positions, Dr. Mason brought Bradbury back to Boston, where the two of them, together with a growing group of talented and interested musicians and composers, led in the development of music for children and young people for the Churches and Sunday Schools of the expanding Republic. Bradbury's part in this movement was a vital and important one, and a study of the hymnals and songbooks of many denominations today reveals that there are about as many original Bradbury tunes in these books as those from any other composer, living or dead.

In 1863, Mr. Bradbury discovered a poem that a British Methodist local preacher, Edward Mote, had written in 1834. Mote had been walking up the cobblestones of Holborn in London when two lines suddenly flashed into his mind, "On Christ The Solid Rock I Stand, All Other Ground Is Sinking Sand". He wrote them down immediately, and added to them before retiring that night. He was so thrilled with the response to his poem that he had copies printed, and it was in an American religious paper that the composer discovered them, set them to music, and gave Christendom the rousing gospel song, "On Christ The Solid Rock I Stand". Let us sing this song together.

—— —— —— —— —— —— —— ——

Two years after Rev. Joseph H. Gilmore wrote the stanzas of his song on the Twenty-Third Psalm, "He Leadeth Me", in March, 1862, Bradbury found them in a Baptist publication, added a lilting Chorus to his original tune, and set the Churches to singing "He Leadeth Me, O Blessed Thought!" Let us sing it together now.

—— —— —— —— —— —— —— ——

In like manner Bradbury had composed the music for a blind British preacher-poet's poem, "Sweet Hour Of Prayer", in 1859. The English clergyman, Rev. William Walford, had written his lines in 1842 and given a copy to an American friend who had sent them in to a metropolitan newspaper, and set them to music. Let us sing now one stanza of this lovely gospel hymn "Sweet Hour Of Prayer", one of the few Bradbury successes that did not have a Chorus or Refrain.

—— —— —— —— —— —— —— ——

It was Mr. Bradbury, who, that very same year, 1859, composed the music for Dorothy Thrupp's poem written in 1836, which was also inspired by the Twenty-third Psalm, "Saviour, Like A Shepherd Lead Us." Let us sing this song at this time.

—— —— —— —— —— —— —— ——

From the prolific musical pen of this talented man came the music for the sacred song that is known to and loved by Christian children the world over. In fact, one could almost affirm that is the most popular children's song in all the world, "Jesus Loves Me". He found the words in a popular novel "Say And Seal" which Anna and Susan Warner had published a few years earlier, and when he set it to music, he little dreamed that it would become so famous that at one time it was even referred to as "the national hymn of China".

Since we expect the children of the congregation to sing our grown-up hymns and songs, let us now join with them as we sing one of Mr. Bradbury's finest tunes, "Jesus Loves Me, This I Know".

———————————

Mr. Bradbury and his brother went into the piano-building business, and Bradbury pianos flooded the New England as well as the Atlantic seaboard states, but he continued to create music in addition to his business responsibilities, and from his pen came two tunes that will live as long as Christians commemorate the sufferings of their Lord, and invite sinners to accept Him as their personal Saviour. The first one is the tune "Olive's Brow" which he composed in 1853 for William Tappan's passion hymn "Tis Midnight And On Olive's Brow". (This may be sung as a solo or choral selection here.) The second is the most impressive and effective invitation hymn in all hymnody, the tune "Woodworth" which Bradbury composed in 1849 for Charlotte Elliott's poem "Just As I Am Without One Plea". As we sing this beautiful hymn, remember that the music came from the soul of the same man who gave us "Jesus Loves Me" and "On Christ The Solid Rock I Stand", and that the hymns and songs which Mr. Bradbury set to music continue to teach us that Jesus Loves, Jesus Leads, Jesus Listens, Jesus Endures, Jesus Suffers and Jesus Receives.

———————————

Among the giants of British hymnody one finds the name of the Anglican clergyman Rev. Henry Francis Lyte (1793-1847) the tubercular minister who spent most of his active years serving the congregation in the fishing village of Lower Brixham, Devonshire, England. It was during the quarter of a century he labored among these humble people that he wrote and published his book "The Spirit Of The Psalms" in 1834, and it was from this original collection that his majestic hymn on Psalm 103, "Praise My Soul The King Of Heaven", found its way into the hearts and hymnals of subsequent generations. In fact, when the future Queen Elizabeth II of England was asked to select the hymns to be sung when she was married to Prince Phillip, one of her choices was Lyte's splendid hymn inspired by Psalm 103. Let us sing together, to the stirring strains of blind Henry Smart's tune "Regent Square", a stanza of Lyte's great hymn.

— — — — — — — — —

Lyte had undergone a remarkable change of heart ten years prior to the publication of his monumental collection of original hymns and poems. Feeling frustrated in his personal spiritual life and finding himself spiritually unfit to serve his God or his fellow-men, he had visited a dying clergyman, only to discover that he had had more to gain from their conversation than to give to it. Out of the "conversion" or "spiritual re-awakening" that resulted from that visit, he penned the stanzas of his autobiographical hymn, "Jesus, I My Cross Have Taken". As we sing this hymn together, remember that it was in the spirit of these lines that the clergyman lived out the remaining years of his active earthly ministry. Let us now sing "Jesus, I My Cross Have Taken, All To Leave And Follow Thee".

— — — — — — — — —

It was in 1847, just a few weeks before his untimely death, that Lyte, his frail body wracked with physical pain, administered communion to his people for the last time. As he packed up his belongings and prepared to take a trip to the south of France in what proved to be a final futile search for good health, he discovered some stanzas that he had written nearly a score of years earlier while sitting at the bedside of a dying parishioner. That afternoon in September, 1847, he reworked his stanzas and read them to his family. They were the stanzas that we know as our hymn "Abide With Me". Within six weeks the preacher-poet was dead, passing away at the foot of the Maritime Alps in southern France. On his gravestone there are his own words,

Heaven's morning breaks and earth's vain shadows flee;
In life, in death, O Lord, Abide with me.

Before we sing this hymn together, let us recall that Lyte's faith moved in these three directions: Praise Of God, "Praise My Soul The King Of Heaven"; Surrender To God, "Jesus,

I My Cross Have Taken"; and Trust in God, "Abide With Me". With that in mind, let us now sing this wonderful hymn from the pen of this remarkable man, "Abide With Me".

———————————

An entirely different kind of hero of the hymnal was an American Baptist clergyman, musician, poet and composer, Rev. Robert Lowry (1826-1899). While his stanzas are hardly in the same class as the exalted poems of Henry Lyte or Baring-Gould, nevertheless, they have been used of God to inspire and instruct His children and to assist them in growing in the Christian life. Lowry was especially interested in the boys and girls of his congregations, and shared in the conviction that congregational singing would be greatly enhanced if poets and composers prepared their stanzas and tunes so that literate adults and young people who could read could sing the stanzas, while adding Choruses or Refrains which the little children could quickly memorize and sing along with the others. With that in mind, Lowry took Rev. Isaac Watts stirring hymn "Come We That Love The Lord", wrote his own lilting tune to supplant the stately cadences of the hymn tune "St. Thomas" and then added a Chorus which probably would have made Dr. Watts turn over in his grave, for it contained these words to the poet's own tune:

We're marching to Zion, Beautiful, beautiful Zion,
We're marching upward to Zion, The beautiful city of God.
While Watts never said any such thing, Lowry's new music and Chorus enabled many to sing "Come We That Love The Lord" who had never heard of it before. Let us now sing Isaac Watts as edited, altered and added to by Robert Lowry, "We're Marching To Zion".

———————————

It was while he was serving as pastor of Hanson Place Baptist Church, Brooklyn, New York that one of his members, Mrs. Annie S. Hawks, handed him some simple couplets which she had written one morning in 1872 while performing her household chores, words which her pastor set to music that very same year, adding, in the custom of the day, a

Chorus of his own, and giving to the world the beautiful gospel hymn, "I Need Thee Every Hour". The poet said of her stanzas later, "My poem was prophetic rather than expressive of my own experience, and I do not understand why it so touched the great throbbing heart of humanity. It was not until long years after, when the shadow of a great loss fell over my way, that I understood something of the comforting in the words I had been permitted to write in my hours of sweet security and peace." With that in mind let us sing together the devotional hymn, "I Need Thee Every Hour".

— — — — — — — —

Dr. Lowry, a one-time professor of rhetoric at his Alma Mater, Bucknell University, once said, "I would rather preach a gospel sermon than write a hymn". Strangely enough, he is remembered today for his hymns rather than his sermons. It was when the good pastor was visiting in the home of one of his parishioners where sudden and unexpected sorrow had been a recent visitor, that he was asked by the bereaved mother, "Pastor, we have parted at the river of death. Will we meet again by the river of life?" He assured her that she and her loved ones whom she had "loved long since and lost awhile" would surely meet "at the river of life that flows by the throne of God", reading to her some words from Revelation 22:1. It was later that same afternoon in 1864 that he wrote the words and music of his famous gospel song, "Shall We Gather At The River?" to give poetic utterance to his profound conviction that "in the Father's house of many mansions", this dear one would meet her beloved children again. As we sing together this gospel song which Mr. Lowry captioned "Mutual Recognition In The Hereafter", let us remember that it has nothing whatsoever to do with baptism by immersion, but was written by a consecrated minister to comfort one of the heart-broken members of his congregation, and is his own musical witness to his faith in the immortality of the soul.

— — — — — — — —

This versatile Baptist minister was also the author and composer of one of the most popular "tear-jerkers" of his day, a song inspired, like "Shall We Gather At The River?" by a question asked him by an anxious member whose boy had run away from home. His poetic response was the last-century favorite "Where Is My Wandering Boy Tonight?" It was in 1875 that he set one of prolific Fanny Crosby's finest hymns to music, "All The Way My Saviour Leads Me". (Here a soloist may sing one stanza of this gospel hymn. If the congregation knows it by heart, they may be invited to sing that first stanza instead.)

———————————

Lowry's finest hymntune was composed in 1871, his forty-fifth year, for a poem by Sylvanus Phelps which began with this stanza:

Saviour, Thy dying love Thou gavest me, Nor should I aught with-hold, Dear Lord from Thee;

In love my soul would bow, My heart fulfill its vow; Some offering bring Thee now, Something for Thee.

This is still one of the best consecration hymns in any hymnal, and as we sing it together, let us not forget the fact that it came from the pen of the same minister who composed the rousing tune to "We're Marching To Zion" as well as the famous popular hit of yesteryear, "Where Is My Wandering Boy Tonight?"

———————————

On the death of William Bradbury in 1868, Rev. Mr. Lowry was selected to take his place as composer-editor by the Bigelow and Main Company, and in that capacity he edited many of their popular Sunday School songbooks, one collection, "Pure Gold", selling more than a million copies. Rev. Charles Wesley wrote the most majestic Easter hymn in the English language, "Christ The Lord Is Risen Today, Alleluia", but it was this American Baptist divine who was privileged to write and compose the most stirring gospel song of the Resurrection, the words and music of "Christ Arose", with its dramatic Refrain, which the children could easily memorize and sing with the adults and young people:

Up from the grave He arose, With a mighty triumph o'er
   His foes;
He arose a victor from the dark domain And He lives for-
   ever with His saints to reign;
He arose, He arose, Hallelujah, Christ arose!!

This musical affirmation of our faith in the reality of the
Easter story is a fitting song with which to conclude our
Hymn Festival on Heroes of the Hymnal. Let us rise and
sing together all three stanzas and Chorus of Rev. Robert
Lowry's gospel hymn, "Christ Arose!"

———————————

(A dramatic true hymn story such as that which inspired
"Stand Up, Stand Up For Jesus" or "It Is Well With My
Soul" may be used as a concluding message, if time permits.
These narratives are among the fifty hymn stories included
in this author's collection entitled "Living Stories Of Famous
Hymns" W. A. Wilde Company; 1955; $2.)

HEROINES OF THE HYMNAL

Anne Steele: Father Of Mercies, In Thy Word
Cecil Frances Alexander: There Is A Green Hill Far
Away
Jesus Calls Us
Annie Sherwood Hawks: I Need Thee Every Hour
Elizabeth Payson Prentiss: More Love To Thee
Elizabeth Cecelia Clephane: Beneath The Cross Of Jesus
The Ninety And Nine
Phoebe Cary: One Sweetly Solemn Thought
Katharine Lee Bates: America The Beautiful
Charlotte Elliott: Just As I Am, Without One Plea
Frances Ridley Havergal: True-Hearted, Whole-Hearted
Lord, Speak To Me That I
May Speak
Golden Harps Are Sounding
I Gave My Life For Thee
Another Year Is Dawning
Take My Life And Let It Be

Anyone who is tempted to believe that all the religions of
the world are equal and that there is really not much differ-
ence between God's revelation in Jesus Christ and the religious teachings of the other leading religions of the world
has but to examine the Hymnals of Christianity to discover
there what Jesus has done for womankind the world over.
In no other major religion of the world does woman enjoy
the place she enjoys as a Christian, for, as a Christian, she
has been permitted to express herself in the same manner,
moved by the same motives, and utilizing the same wide
variety of poetic meters as the men, and in the Hymnals and

35

Songbooks of the Christian faith alone do we find her hymns and songs alongside those of the men, oftentimes surpassing them in quality and eclipsing them in quantity. Thus, some of the most popular as well as the most beloved of the songs of Christendom are the creations of devoted, consecrated and enlightened women, and it has been one of the glories of the Christian Church that she has not denied them this honor nor questioned their right to this exalted place of privilege. When the Mohammedans, Confucians, Hindus, Animists and other religions of the world begin to permit their women to occupy a similar place in their societies and encourage them to express their emotions and convictions in hymns of praise that will become the common property of all believers, then Christians will be able to boast that the influence of Christ has permeated even the "inner sanctums" of those groups which boast of being non-Christian faiths. As we sing together these hymns from nine Heroines of the Hymnal, remember, we could just as easily have selected nine different women or even ninety-nine or possibly even nine-hundred, so great has been their contribution to ecumenical hymnody reflecting so great a love they have possessed individually for their Saviour and Lord. Out of her joys and sorrows, her victories and defeats, her tragedies and triumphs have come the hymns and songs we will sing and hear during this service.

————————

The first of what became a noble line of English-speaking hymn writers was a native of Hampshire, England, Miss Anne Steele (1716-1778), who published most of her finest poems under the pseudonym "Theodosia", in a collection entitled "Poems On Subjects Chiefly Devotional" in 1760, the author's forty-fourth year. Inspired by her example, and the success which attended her efforts, other women began to write and publish their own sacred poems, their labours being crowned by the works of such pre-eminent hymn and song writers as England's Frances Ridley Havergal and America's Fanny Crosby. Miss Steele lost her fiance by drowning the day before their scheduled wedding, and, out of her anguish and grief, she was led to pen these beautiful and revealing lines:

Father, whate'er of earthly bliss, Thy sovereign will denies,
Accepted at Thy throne of grace, Let this petition rise:
 Give me a calm, a thankful heart, From every murmur free;
 The blessings of Thy grace impart, And let me live to thee.

One of her best hymns is a poetic tribute to her own love for The Holy Scriptures, and begins with this stanza:

 Father of mercies, in Thy Word What endless glory shines;
 Forever be Thy Name adored, For these celestial lines.

Let us sing this hymn together. (These lines may be sung to any familiar Common Meter tune, preferably "Naomi" or "Beatitudo". The first stanza of each of these hymns may be sung as solos if the congregation is not acquainted with either.)

——— ——— ——— ——— ———

In the next century the wife of the primate of the Anglican Church in Ireland, Mrs. Cecil Frances Humphreys Alexander, wrote herself into immortality with a series of hymns based upon various phrases of The Apostles' Creed, written originally for a group of children in her Sunday School class.

For the phrase "God, the Father Almighty, Maker of Heaven and Earth" she wrote "All Things Bright And Beautiful"; for "Born of the Virgin Mary" she wrote "Once in Royal David's City" and for "Crucified, Dead and Buried" she wrote the lovely passion hymn "There Is A Green Hill Far Away". As set to music by the American composer George Stebbins, this is still an impressive sacred song. Let us sing together the first stanza and Chorus of Mrs. Alexander's hymn to Mr. Stebbins tune.

——— ——— ——— ——— ———

Following a sermon she heard her distinguished husband preach on the life, ministry and death of Moses, Mrs. Alexander (1818-1895) wrote the majestic poem "The Burial Of Moses" which is still one of the noblest in all English literature. Later when her preacher-husband asked her to write another poem with which he could conclude a St. Andrew's Day sermon, she wrote her wonderful hymn "Jesus

37

Calls Us, O'er The Tumult" in 1852. Although the stanza about St. Andrew is no longer included in our hymnals, her other four stanzas are loved the world over. Let us sing from the pen of this prolific poet, "Jesus Calls Us".

———————————

A thirty-seven year old Brooklyn, New York, housewife, Mrs. Annie Sherwood Hawks (1835-1918) who was a member of the Hanson Place Baptist Church, wrote some couplets one morning as she did her house-work, and the following Sunday she showed her simple stanzas to her pastor, the preacher-composer, Rev. Robert Lowry. He took them home, set them to lilting music, added a Chorus of his own in the custom of the day and that very same year, 1872, gave us the hymn "I Need Thee Every Hour". Let us sing this hymn together, remembering, as we do, the circumstances in which it was born.

———————————

Sixteen years before Mrs. Hawks penned her little lines, the wife of a Seminary Professor in nearby New York City, Mrs. Elizabeth Payson Prentiss (1818-1878) overcame her personal grief at the loss of two of her little sons when she applied to her own heart the advice her distinguished Presbyterian minister husband had given others on similar occasions, "Love alone can keep the soul from going blind". Praying that God would so fill her with love that there would be no room in her heart for doubt or despair, this talented author, novelist and poet wrote the story of her spiritual pilgrimage in her noblest hymn, a prayer for inner peace that began
More love to Thee, O Christ, More love to Thee!
Hear Thou the prayer I make, On bended knee;
This is my earnest plea, More love, O Christ, to Thee.
Although written in 1856, the poet's thirty-eighth year, her stanzas were not discovered until more than a decade later, whereupon William H. Doane, the Cincinnati business man who collaborated with Fanny Crosby on many of her best hymns and gospel songs, set them to music. As we sing "More Love To Thee" let us remember that today Dr. Prentiss' advice is still as true as it was when he first spoke

38

it over a century ago, "Love alone can keep the soul from going blind". Let us sing this devotional prayer together.

———————————

Three years after the Scottish poet, Miss Elizabeth Cecelia Clephane (1830-1869) died at thirty-nine, Rev. Mr. Arnot, editor of a religious journal "The Family Treasury" who knew of Miss Clephane's sacred writings, published two of her finest poems in his magazine within a black-edged square, and entitled them "Breathings From The Border". Thus were her two finest hymns preserved for posterity, for those poems were "Beneath The Cross Of Jesus" and "The Ninety And Nine". The first hymn was her own testimony of faith, and when sung to the tune "St. Christopher" composed by Frederick Maker in 1881, is as deeply devotional a hymn on the Passion and Atonement of our Lord as any from the pen of Watts, Wesley or Heber. The American song-leader Ira D. Sankey discovered "The Ninety And Nine" in a British newspaper while travelling with the evangelist Dwight L. Moody on an evangelistic tour of the British Isles, and set it to music spontaneously as a sacred solo before several thousand worshippers in Edinburgh, Scotland one night in 1874. It proved to be the finest tune Sankey ever composed. After *(name of singer)* sings "The Ninety And Nine" as a sacred solo, we will sing together Miss Clephane's hymn "Beneath The Cross Of Jesus".

———————————

Phoebe Cary, an American poet, was just twenty-eight years old one memorable Sunday afternoon in 1852 when she climbed to the third-floor apartment she shared with her sister in New York City, and talked with her and their landlady about their desire for a home all their very own. Out of that conversation came her finest hymn, the stanzas known as "One Sweetly Solemn Thought". This is still an effective congregational hymn on heaven, although in recent years it has also become a popular sacred solo and choral anthem. (Here let these stanzas be sung either as a solo, choral number or congregational hymn.)

It was in 1892 that a Wellesley professor, thirty-three year old Miss Katharine Lee Bates, the daughter of a Congregational clergyman, visited the Columbian Exposition in Chicago and then travelled farther west with a group of fellow-teachers, visiting enroute, the city of Denver, Colorado, nearby Colorado Springs, and even climbing to the top of snow-covered Pike's Peak. That well-remembered evening she was inspired to express her experiences in a poem that was eventually to take its rightful place alongside "America" and "The Star Spangled Banner" as one of the finest patriotic poems in our nation's history, for she had written the four stanzas of the hymn we know now as "America The Beautiful". Set some years later to a stirring tune "Materna" which the Newark, N. J. organist, Samuel Ward, had originally composed for the hymn "O Mother Dear, Jerusalem" (hence the tune's Latin name, which means "Mother"), this is still as noble a poetic statement of true Americanism as any native has produced. It is significant that not only is it a lofty patriotic poem, but it is also a worthy Christian hymn. Let us sing together now "America The Beautiful".

— — — — — — — —

Turning again to England, we find the name of Charlotte Elliott (1789-1871), the "Sunbeam" of Brighton, England, who is well-known the world over for her autobiographical hymn which has become one of our finest "invitation hymns", "Just As I Am Without One Plea". In 1822, Dr Cesar Malan, a renowned Swiss minister, musician and hymn-writer, had said to Miss Elliott, the thirty-three year old rebellious daughter of his host at Brighton, "One becomes a Christian, Charlotte, by coming to Christ and saying, 'Jesus I come to Thee, just as I am.'" On the fourteenth anniversary of that conversation, and after a radical change of heart that had made a new woman of her, Charlotte received a letter from Dr. Malan. Recalling his historic words, and grieving because she could not help her preacher-brother Henry with a bazaar he was promoting that day for nearby St. Mary's School for Girls, she wrote the stanzas of this superb hymn. Henry Venn Elliott later confessed that Charlotte accomplished more good for Christ by means of that one hymn than he had been privileged to accomplish in a lifetime of preaching and pastoral work. The American composer, William Bradbury, set these stanzas to music in 1849, and it would be almost impossible to number those men and women, young people and boys and girls who have dedicated themselves to Christ and His Church during the singing of "Just As I Am". Let us sing together several stanzas of this wonderful hymn.

——— —— —— —— ——

English hymnody came to full flower in the poems and tunes of another remarkable woman, Miss Frances Ridley Havergal (1836-1879), a devout Christian, who, like Charlotte Elliott, suffered from ill health most of her adult years. In spite of that physical handicap, Miss Havergal wrote some of the most active hymns and composed some of the most thrilling tunes in all hymnody. Her lines abound in one-syllable verbs, while her stanzas possess a movement and vigor that belied their author's actual physical condition. One of her finest hymns was set to music by George Stebbins. We know it as "True-Hearted, Whole-Hearted". Let us sing one stanza of this stirring hymn now.

——— —— —— —— ——

It was this same unusual and talented woman who wrote the hymn "Lord, Speak To Me That I May Speak" and lived out in her own brief life the answered petitions of this prayer. Let us sing a stanza of this hymn together. (This hymn may be sung to several different Long Meter tunes, such as "Gratitude" by Paul Bost, and "Cannonbury" arranged from a "Night Song" by Robert Schumann.)

——— —— —— —— ——

From the pen of Frances Ridley Havergal came the thrilling tune "Hermas" which she composed for her own stanzas "Golden Harps Are Sounding". Today many people sing the Easter hymn "Welcome, Happy Morning" to Miss Havergal's tune, but as we listen to it played, note that it possesses the same dynamic spirit as the stanzas of the hymns we have just been singing. (Here let the organist play the hymntune "Hermas". If either hymn mentioned above is familiar, the congregation, a soloist or the Choir may sing it instead.)

———————————

Miss Havergal's very first hymn was a poem so simple that the poet threw the paper on which she had just written it into the fireplace. As the fire crept toward the sheet, she was led to snatch it out and preserve it. When she read it to a woman in an alms house later that day, and saw her reaction and response, she felt God had spared it for His own greater glory. As set to music by Philip Bliss, this hymn is "I Gave My Life For Thee". Let us sing one stanza now. (If this is unfamiliar, let it be sung as a solo, duet or choral selection.)

———————————

Miss Havergal wrote stanzas and verses for greeting cards, and one of the poems she wrote originally for a New Year's card has become our splendid New Year's hymn, "Another Year Is Dawning". Although these lines are sung to many different tunes, let us sing them to the familiar strains of "Aurelia", the tune we generally associate with "The Church's One Foundation". (In some Hymnals, this hymn is printed in four-line stanzas, and in others in eight-line stanzas. In the event it is printed as four-line stanzas, let the congregation sing two stanzas of the words to one of the music.)

———————————

This poet's finest hymn was penned just five years before her untimely death at the age of forty-three in 1879, and is our hymn of dedication, "Take My Life And Let It Be, Consecrated, Lord, To Thee". Dated February 4, 1874, she wrote it as she prayed for the conversion of several house guests who were spending a weekend with her family at Areley House. No finer hymn of personal dedication has ever been written. Let us conclude our Hymn Festival on Heroines Of The Hymnal with Miss Havergal's hymn, "Take My Life And Let It Be". (Let these stanzas be sung to the tune with which the local congregation is most familiar.)

ISAAC WATTS
1674-1748
Singing A New Song

Behold The Glories Of The Lamb
Alas! And Did My Saviour Bleed (At The Cross)
Come We That Love The Lord (Marching To Zion)
Joy To The World
O God Our Help In Ages Past
Jesus Shall Reign
Hush, My Dear, Lie Still And Slumber
Am I A Soldier Of The Cross?
There Is A Land Of Pure Delight
When I Survey The Wondrous Cross

One of the most unusual and remarkable names in the entire history of Christian hymnody is that of Isaac Watts. This little clergyman of the Church of England single-handedly revolutionized the congregational singing habits of Christendom, convincing believers by the excellence of his own original poems that God had not stopped singing when David died! By the quality as well as the quantity of his own hymns he set the standard by which sacred stanzas were to be judged for several generations.

Isaac, the grandson of a renowned British Naval Commander, Thomas Watts, and the son of Enoch Watts, Sr., a deacon in the local Congregational Church, was born in Southampton, England, July 17, 1674. His father was imprisoned on more than one occasion for publicly declaring some of his religious convictions which happened not to coincide with the views then held by Britian's ruling family. Consequently he became quite familiar with the inside as well as the outside of the local jail. During the months of his imprisonment, his wife, with baby Isaac in her arms, often came to the prison gate, there to sit on a nearby stone and sing Psalms with Enoch who would join in from the other side of the jailhouse wall. Thus did little Isaac learn not only the Psalms of David but also some of the crude versifications which enthusiastic but untutored poets were then trying to foist upon the Church. Very early, too, the young lad tried his own hand at making verses, much to the delight of his parents and to the chagrin of his older brother Enoch. At seven he entered this couplet as his contribution in a contest for the prize of a farthing offered by his mother to the child producing the best bit of original verse:

"I write not for a farthing, but to try, How I your farthing authors can outvie! !" Needless to say, he won the prize! The type of hymns then being sung in public worship would naturally catch the eye as well as the ear of so talented a young poet and soon Isaac was examining the hymnals of his day with a critical rather than a sympathetic mind. What he read and heard discouraged, dismayed and disgusted him.

"The Psalms of David deserve better treatment," he would say to his brother, only to hear the older lad reply, as he nodded in agreement, "Why don't you do something about it, Isaac?" One that particularly irked him was someone's inspired lines based upon Psalm 133:2:

'Tis like the precious ointment down Aaron's beard did go; Down Aaron's beard it downward went, His garment's
skirts unto. (Selah)

Soon the two brothers became so bold that they actually criticized these ridiculous hymns in the presence of their parents. Deacon Watts could hardly believe his Congregational ears. "Are you daring to pronounce judgment upon the hymns we use in public worship?" he thundered. Instead of frightening Isaac half out of his wits, his father's question only stirred him into action. "Yes, father," the lad replied. "They are not fit for use in divine worship." "Well, if you don't like these hymns, let me see one which you have written that can compare with those we are now using," the stern father added. That gave Isaac the opening he had been praying for. "I have one which I have written which I am sure is better, father," he explained. "Would you like to hear it?" Enoch Watts, Sr. gazed at his young second son and said, "Yes; I would very much like to hear it." As Isaac reached into his pocket for the manuscript, he explained, "Instead of basing my hymn upon one of the Psalms of David in the Old Testament, I have taken my inspiration from the Revelation of St. John in the New Testament." Then opening the piece of paper, he continued, "This hymn is based upon Revelation 5, verses 6 through 10." With that, he began reading aloud his first hymn:

1. Behold the glories of the Lamb, Amidst His father's
        throne;
    Prepare new honors for His Name, And songs before
        unknown.
2. Let elders worship at His feet, The Church adore
        around;
    With vials full of odors sweet, And harps of sweetest
        sound.
3. Those are the prayers of all the saints, And these the
        hymns they raise;
    Jesus is kind to our complaints, He loves to hear our
        praise.

He paused, glanced at his brother and then looked over at his parents. His father's expression was not as stern as it had been a few moments before, and it was evident that he was both pleased and bewildered at Isaac's creation. "Proceed," he said with parental dignity. Isaac continued reading:

4. Now to the Lamb that once was slain, Be endless bless-
        ings paid;
    Salvation, glory, joy remain, Forever on Thy head.
5. Thou hast redeemed our souls with blood, Hast set the
        prisoner free;
    Hast made us kings and priests to God, And we shall
        reign with Thee.

6. The worlds of nature and of grace, Are put beneath Thy
        power;
    Then shorten these delaying days, And bring the prom-
        ised hour.

His father rose, walked over to the young man's side,
placed a loving arm tenderly upon his shoulder and said,
"I've been a bit hasty, Isaac, and I ask your forgiveness.
You have written a noble hymn, and one I will be proud to
introduce to our congregation next Sunday morning." While
we do not know to what Common Meter tune this hymn was
first sung the following Sunday morning, suffice it to say that
the gifted young man was asked to prepare another hymn
for the next Sunday and the next, requests he filled for two-
hundred and twenty-two consecutive Sundays. When he completed his education, he took Holy Orders and preached his
first sermon as a full-fledged clergyman when he was twenty-
four. For ten years he served as the assistant and then as the
minister of the Independent Church in Mark Lane, London,
continuing all the time to produce more and more original
hymns for the glory of God and the worship of man. When
he was thirty-one years of age, he published his first collection of original hymns, this being followed two years later,
in 1707, with his "Hymns And Spiritual Songs", a volume
that eventually contained three parts: Part I, Collected from
the Scriptures, 150 Hymns; Part II, Composed on Divine
Subjects, 170 Hymns; Part III, Prepared for the Lord's
Supper, 45 Hymns. Hymn 9 of Part II, entitled "Godly
Sorrow Arising from the Sufferings of Christ" is his majestic
passion hymn "Alas! And Did My Saviour Bleed":

1. Alas! and did my Saviour bleed! And did my Soverign
        die?
    Would he devote that sacred head, For such a worm as I?
2. Was it for crimes that I had done, He groaned upon the
        tree?
    Amazing pity, grace unknown, And love beyond degree!
3. Well might the sun in darkness hide, And shut his glories
        in,

46

When God, the mighty maker, died, For man, the creature's sin.

4. Thus might I hide my blushing face, While his dear cross appears,
   Dissolve my heart in thankfulness, And melt mine eyes in tears.

5. But drops of grief can ne'er repay, The debt of love I owe:
   Here, Lord, I give myself away: Tis all that I can do.

To dull the sharp rapier of Watt's theology, editors have taken such liberty in altering his original lines that today some worshippers sing:
"Would he devote that sacred head, For sinners such as I?"
while still others go a step farther and sing:
"Would he devote that sacred head, For such a one as I?"
I wrote my own rebuttal in a four-line poem that contains these lines:

It used to seem absurd to me, To sing of 'such a worm as I',
Until I saw an ugly worm, Become a gorgeous butterfly!

Possibly Watts' figures of speech were actually closer to the heart of the Gospel than those alterations of his critics! The change wrought in the human heart whereby a sinner dies that a saint may be born has its parallel in nature when a worm dies that a butterfly may be born! This hymn is generally sung to the tune "Martyrdom (Avon)" composed by Hugh Wilson in 1825. (The Leader may here invite the congregation to sing several stanzas of this hymn to this stirring tune.)

———————————————

In recent years, composers have taken some of Watts' dignified stanzas and set them to lilting gospel tunes. Then, in order to interest the children, they have added a "Chorus" or "Refrain" to the original stanzas on the theory that the adults who could read would sing the verses with the children joining in on the easily memorized Choruses. With that in mind, composer R. E. Hudson took "Alas! And Did My Saviour Bleed" and made it the gospel song "At The Cross". While the words of the "Refrain'" were not from Isaac

Watts' pen, let us sing a stanza or two of this gospel song, remembering that it was originally a majestic passion hymn.

———————————

Later Rev. Robert Lowry, a Brooklyn Baptist clergyman, did the same thing with Watts' Short Meter hymn "Come, We That Love The Lord" (Hymn 30, of Part II), and made it into the gospel song, "Marching To Zion", adding the "Chorus" himself. By way of contrast, let us sing one stanza of this hymn to the hymn tune "St. Thomas", and then sing a stanza and "Chorus" as composed by Robert Lowry.

This strange innovation came as an indirect result of the influence of Negro Spirituals, in which the theme of the stanzas was repeated over and over again, many times to the same tune, in what we now call a "Refrain" or "Chorus". Incidentally, this is a typically American contribution to hymnody, for better or for worse. The great hymns of Watts, Wesley, Heber and Doddridge had no such appendages. Today the pendulum seems to have swung to the opposite extreme. Whereas our grandfathers sang stanzas with no Choruses, today their grandchildren sing Choruses with no stanzas!

———————————

In 1719 Watts brought out his monumental work, "The Psalms of David, Imitated in the Language of The New Testament, and applied to the Christian State and Worship", a collection of 150 hymns based on each of the 150 Psalms. His free poetic rendering of Psalm 98, in which he read into the Old Testament promise the New Testament fulfilment, is now our joyous Christmas carol "Joy To The World". Sung to a theme arranged from Handel's "Messiah", this is as glorious a Christmas hymn as exists in all Christian literature. Let us sing together "Joy To The World".

———————————

Although he had written the noble lines in 1714, shortly before the death of England's Queen Anne, when the nation was troubled over her successor to the throne, "Our God, Our Help In Ages Past" was not published until 1719 as the hymn inspired by Psalm 90: "Lord, thou hast been our dwelling place in all generations; Before the mountains were brought forth or ever thou hadst formed the earth and the world, from everlasting to everlasting, thou art God." It was John Wesley who altered the first word, changing "Our" to "O", but as sung to William Croft's tune "St Anne", composed in 1708, this is as majestic a hymn as any that came from Watts' pen during his long life of seventy-four years. Let us sing "O God, Our Help In Ages Past".

— — — — — — — —

The shortest chapter in the Bible, Psalm 117, inspired the poet to write "From All That Dwell Below The Skies", which also appeared for the first time in this monumental volume of 1719. (A stanza or two of this hymn may be sung here, to the tune "Duke Street", preceded by the reading of the two verses of this briefest of all Psalms.)

— — — — — — — —

Just as he took Psalm 98 and made a Christmas carol out of it, so also did he take Psalm 72 and, in the same volume, make of it the first great missionary hymn of modern times, "Jesus Shall Reign Where'er The Sun". This hymn was first published in 1719 and exactly one-hundred years were to pass before Reginald Heber wrote the great missionary hymn of the nineteenth century in 1819, "From Greenland's Icy Mountains". Of his eight original stanzas, several are still in common use. Let us sing "Jesus Shall Reign", remembering that it is the first great missionary hymn of this era, and has been sung for nearly two and a half centuries. (In most Hymnals these lines are sung to John Hatton's tune "Duke Street".)

— — — — — — — —

While Watts never married, one admirer, Miss Elizabeth Singer, wrote him a letter in which she confessed that she had fallen in love with him while reading his hymns and poems. Elated at the thought of ending his bachelor's existence, he responded and a meeting was arranged. The young lady, however, took but one disappointed look at the little clergyman "only five feet tall, with a sallow face, hooked nose, prominent cheek bones, small eyes and a deathlike color", blushed unashamedly and asked to be excused. When asked later why she refused his proposal of marriage, she replied, "I admired the jewel but not the casket." Nevertheless, the poet, who shortly thereafter reputedly wrote a hymn which began:

"How vain are all things here below, How false and yet so fair", wrote one of the loveliest lullabies in all literature:

1. Hush, my dear, lie still and slumber, Holy angels guard thy bed;

    Heavenly blessings without number, Gently falling on thy head.

    Sleep, my babe, thy food and raiment, House and home thy friends provide;

    All without thy care or payment; All thy wants are well supplied.

2. Soft and easy is thy cradle, Coarse and hard thy Saviour lay,

    When his birthplace was a stable, And his softest bed was hay.

    Lo, he slumbers in a manger, Where the hornéd oxen fed;

    Sleep my darling, here's no danger; There's no oxen near thy bed.

These beautiful stanzas are still sung to the tune "Nettleton" which John Wyeth composed about 1813, a tune to which "Come Thou Fount Of Every Blessing" is almost universally sung. (Here a child or a Junior Choir may sing these stanzas to that well-known tune.)

———————————

When Watts suffered a nervous breakdown during his tenth year at Independent Church, his friends, Lord Mayor and Lady Thomas Abney, invited him to recuperate and rest at their London estate. He accepted their gracious invitation, expecting to remain but a few weeks. But the weeks lengthened into months and the months into years. Sir Thomas, concerned about Watts' ill health, offered him the position of Chaplain of his estate, thereby freeing him from pastoral duties and permitting him to devote his time and energy to his creative work. Years later when someone asked Lady Abney how long Dr. Watts had been their guest, she replied, "Thirty-six years". "Is not that a rather lengthy visit?" the inquirer asked. The gracious lady quickly replied, "It is the shortest visit a friend ever paid a friend." While at their home, Watts wrote a volume of sermons, concluding one on I Corinthians 16:13, "Stand fast in the faith — be strong", with his hymn "Am I A Soldier Of The Cross?" one of his rare hymns that contains more questions than answers. Thomas Arne, who composed the tune "Arlington" to which these lines are now sung, will be remembered for his popular patriotic success "Rule Britannia". This hymn tune is an adaptation of one of the minuets he included in his opera "Artaxerxes" in 1762, being published as a hymn tune twenty-two years later under the editorship of Rev. Ralph Harrison. Let us sing "Am I A Soldier Of The Cross?"

———————

During the American Revolutionary War, the Rev. James Caldwell was pastor of the Presbyterian Church in Elizabeth, New Jersey, when a group of British soldiers marched from their headquarters on Staten Island to capture and burn the town of Springfield, New Jersey, in May 1780. Among the innocent civilians who were killed during this action was the clergyman's wife who was hit by a stray bullet while crouching in a corner of their home trying to shield their baby from harm. Three weeks after this initial action the enemy attempted another sortie, but General Washington's militia got word of it and his soldiers were all lined up on the ground ready to give battle in what was later called "The Battle of Springfield" in June 1780. When the defenders discovered a tragic shortage of wadding for their guns, the minister hurried to his Church, picked up an armful of hymnals, rushed to the scene of impending battle and handed out the books to the plucky soldiers with the admonition, "Give 'em Watts, boys; Give 'em Watts!" Using Watts for wadding, they held their ground against the enemy and won the victory they so well deserved. In less than three-quarters of a century the name of Isaac Watts had become synonymous with that of the Hymnal itself!

His great hymn on heaven, "There Is A Land Of Pure Delight", was included in his 1707 volume. The lines, replete with Scriptural imagery, are sung today to the tune "Varina" from the pen of the prolific composer of many popular Civil War songs, George F. Root (1820-1895). (A stanza of this hymn may be sung here.)

———————————

Hymn 7 of Part III of "Hymns and Spiritual Songs" is a five stanza Long Meter hymn entitled "Crucifixion to the world by the cross of Christ", based upon Galatians 6:14. Four of its stanzas are now considered among the noblest in all Christian hymnody, for they comprise the majestic hymn "When I Survey The Wondrous Cross". Set to the music of a Gregorian chant discovered in Hamburg, Germany and named for that city by composer-arranger Lowell Mason (1792-1872), this hymn is loved and revered the world over, being the favorite hymn of countless Christians in every land in which the Gospel has been preached and sung.

In addition to writing several volumes of hymns and sacred songs, Isaac Watts, who was honored with Doctor's Degrees from the Universities of Aberdeen and Edinburgh, wrote a total of fifty-two books on a wide variety of subjects prior to his death in 1748. While he was buried in London's crowded Bunhill Fields Cemetery, across the street from John Wesley's "City Road Chapel", a monument to his memory was erected elsewhere in London containing this inscription: "In memory of Dr. Isaac Watts and in testimony of the high esteem in which his character and writings are held by the great Christian community of English-speaking people. Of his psalms and hymns it may be predicted 'Ages unborn will make his songs, The joy and labor of their tongues.' He was born at Southampton, July 17, 1674 and died in the seventy-fifth year of his existence, November 25, 1748 after a residence of thirty-six years in the mansion of Sir Thomas Abney which then stood on these grounds." Let us sing in closing all four stanzas of Isaac Watts' greatest hymn, "When I Survey The Wondrous Cross" to the hymn tune "Hamburg" by Lowell Mason.

CHARLES WESLEY
1707-1788
Praise Ye The Lord

Where Shall My Wondering Soul Begin
O For A Thousand Tongues To Sing
Hark, The Herald Angels Sing
Christ The Lord Is Risen Today
Behold The Saviour Of Mankind
Jesus, Lover Of My Soul
Come, O Thou Traveller Unknown
Soldiers Of Christ Arise
And Are We Yet Alive
And Let Our Bodies Part
Blow Ye The Trumpet, Blow
Arise, My Soul, Arise
A Charge To Keep I Have
Love Divine

Rev. Charles Wesley, the son of Rev. Samuel Wesley and his gifted wife, Susannah, and the grandson of Rev. John Wesley, the vicar of White Church, Dorsetshire, England, was born in the Anglican parsonage at Epworth, England, December 18, 1707, the eighteenth of his parent's nineteen children. His older brother, John, the fifteenth Wesley heir, had preceded him in birth by about four and a half years. While John attended Charterhouse School, Charles received his education at Westminster in London. It was Charles who began The Holy Club at Oxford University in 1727, a group his older brother John was to lead when he returned to his Alma Mater as a professor a few years later. The two brothers spent a disappointing year in the colony of

Georgia in the New World at the invitation of General Ogle-
thorpe in 1735, the year of Charles' ordination as a clergyman, both of them being disillusioned, disappointed and disgusted at their inability to do anything whatsoever about
"converting the Indians", their principle reason for making
the perilous journey across the Atlantic in the first place.
Charles returned to England after a few unhappy months,
his brother remaining abroad for another year in order not
to disappoint their sponsors, the Society for the Propagation
of the Gospel in Foreign Parts. During his thirty-first year,
Charles had a marvelous spiritual reawakening, the date of
this remarkable experience being May 20, 1738, on Pentecost, just four days prior to John's famous "heart-warming".
In the joy and ecstacy of that memorable moment, he burst
into song, penning his very first hymn, a lengthy poem of
eight stanzas which began:
Where shall my wondering soul begin? How shall I all to
      heaven aspire?
A slave redeemed from death and sin, A brand plucked from
      eternal fire?
How shall I equal triumphs raise, Or sing my great Deliver-
      er's praise?

In this first stanza of his first hymn Charles notified his
distinguished preacher-brother John, that he, too, was as
much "a brand plucked from the burning" (Zechariah 3:2)
as mother Susannah had told John he was, following the older lad's dramatic last-minute rescue from a fire that destroyed
their Epworth parsonage on February 9, 1709. But once he
began writing sacred verses, they continued to flow "like a
veritable flood" and only his death at the age of eighty-one on
March 29, 1788, finally stilled his fluent and forceful pen.
(Let a soloist sing this stanza, and one or two others if available, to the hymntune "St. Catherine" — Faith Of Our
Fathers.)

———————————

One year after the day which he spoke of as his "spiritual
birthday", Charles Wesley recalled an admonition of his
spiritual mentor, the Moravian clergyman Peter Bohler, who

had once said to him, "If I had a thousand tongues, I would praise Christ with all of them." With that in mind, Wesley wrote an anniversary hymn of eighteen stanzas, the seventh of which contained these lines, now familiar to Methodists the world over:

O for a thousand tongues to sing, My great Redeemer's
      praise;
The glories of my God and King, The triumphs of His grace.

Set to a stirring tune "Azmon," composed by a German musician Carl Glaser in 1828 and arranged as a hymntune by Dr. Lowell Mason in 1839, this is as noble a hymn as exists in all hymnody. Let us sing together several stanzas of Wesley's hymn "O For A Thousand Tongues To Sing."

— — — — — — — —

That very same year, 1739, when he was thirty-two years of age, Charles Wesley wrote his finest Christmas carol, "Hark, The Herald Angels Sing," his opening stanza containing these lines:

Hark, how all the welkin rings, Glory to the King of Kings. ("Welkin" is an old English word meaning "the vault of heaven").

Wesley's co-worker, the renowned evangelist George Whitfield, suggested that the poet change the opening line to read:

Hark, the herald angels sing, Glory to the new-born King.

The poet accepted Whitfield's advice, and thus did this thrilling Christmas hymn come into existence. The German composer Felix Mendelssohn was thirty-two years of age in 1840 when he was commissioned to compose several anthems to be used in connection with an anniversary celebration of Guttenberg's invention of the printing press. A British Doctor of Music, William H. Cummings, took the music of Mendelssohnn's "Festgesang #7" and arranged it as a hymntune for Wesley's Advent hymn in 1855, giving to Christendom one of her most joyous and exciting Christmas hymns. Let us sing together a stanza of "Hark, The Herald Angels Sing".

— — — — — — — —

That very same year also saw Charles Wesley writing his finest Easter hymn, the universally revered stanzas that begin:

Christ the Lord is risen today, Alleluia; Sons of men and
          angels say, Alleluia;

Raise your joys and triumphs high, Alleluia; Sing ye heavens
          and earth reply, Alleluia.

Had Wesley written only these three hymns during his thirty-second year, he would have placed all of us in his debt. But this was merely the beginning of a long and creative ministry of song that spanned half a century. Let us sing this first stanza to the majestic music of the tune "Lyra Davidica" which first appeared in a London publication in 1708, the name of the actual composer being unknown.

———————

Charles inherited some of his poetic talent from his preacher-father who, at various times and for various reasons, wrote lengthy poems and dedicated them to the currently reigning Monarchs of the British people. In fact, Father Wesley had just put the finishing touches on a new hymn when the fire broke out that destroyed his home in February, 1709. The following day, the badly beset parson managed to find his fire-scarred manuscript among the debris, and the only reason this hymn is now found in some Methodist hymnals is because it came from the pen of prolific Charles Wesley's father, and was a souvenir of the tragic fire that almost cost six-year old John Wesley his life. Father's hymn began:

Behold the Saviour of mankind, Nailed to the shameful tree!
How vast the love that Him inclined, To bleed and die for
          thee!

(Here let a soloist or quartet sing a stanza or two of this hymn to any appropriate Common Meter tune, preferably "Dundee (Windsor)" or a similar tune in a minor key.)

———————

The following year, 1740, when Charles Wesley was a maturing minister of thirty-three, he was privileged to pen what future worshippers were to call the "best hymn" of the six-thousand he was to write, the four forceful stanzas of

"Jesus, Lover Of My Soul". Many fanciful tales have been told about the origin of these stanzas, most of which have no basis in fact. The author had endured the terrors of a violent storm at sea, but that had been four years earlier, in 1736, on his voyage home from Georgia. He had also experienced a mystical and rather miraculous recovery from serious illness, but that had been two years earlier, in 1738. Finally, he had accompanied some condemned felons on their way to the gallows, to assure them of God's forgiving power and of His infinite love. These and other similar experiences converged in 1740 and led him to write his four beautiful stanzas, the first of which is known the world over:

Jesus, lover of my soul, Let me to Thy bosom fly;
While the nearer waters roll, While the tempest still is high.
Hide me, O my Saviour, hide; Till the storm of life is past;
Safe into Thy haven guide, O receive my soul at last.

John thought these stanzas were "sentimental slush", an apt observation from an Oxford Professor whose heart was never "red-hot" but merely "strangely warm", and for some years he vetoed its inclusion in the official hymnals and songbooks of the Methodist people. He yielded to the people's pressures, however, and these four stanzas soon found a permanent place both in the hearts and hymnals of Christendom. The tune "Martyn", to which these lines are universally sung, was originally composed by Simeon Marsh in 1834 for Rev. John Newton's hymn "Mary, To Her Saviour's Tomb, Hastened At The Early Dawn". It was Dr. Thomas Hastings, the author of the hymn "Hail To The Brightness Of Zion's Glad Morning" and the composer of the tune "Toplady" for "Rock Of Ages", who married Marsh's music to Wesley's words, perfecting as beautiful a musical wedding as exists in all hymnody. Let us sing together a stanza of "Jesus Lover Of My Soul" to the familiar strains of the tune "Martyn".

— — — — — — — —

It was in 1741, the year after he wrote "Jesus, Lover Of My Soul", that Charles wrote the majestic stanzas of his hymn "Wrestling Jacob" or "Come, O Thou Traveller Unknown", a hymn which drew from the great Dr. Isaac Watts this tribute, "This hymn is worth all that I myself have written". Remember that Watts was the clergyman who gave to the world such hymns as "Joy To The World", "Alas And Did My Saviour Bleed", "O God Our Help In Ages Past", "Jesus Shall Reign" and "When I Survey The Wondrous Cross". Wesley had often preached on the story of Jacob wrestling with the angel at Peniel from Genesis 32: 24-32, but it was not until that particular year that he felt inspired to put his sermon into song:

Come, O Thou traveller known, Whom still I hold but cannot see;
My company before is gone, And I am left alone with Thee;
With Thee all night I mean to stay, And wrestle till the break of day.

When these fourteen stanzas appeared in a collection the very next year, they were immediately accepted by the Methodist people as among the preacher-poet's finest.

The lilting tune to which some denominations sing these stanzas was originally composed as a joke by a Scotsman named Clarke. He said to a fellow Scot, "I am anxious to compose a good Scots air. How do I go about it?" His friend replied jokingly, "Get a good rhythm, play it on the black keys of the piano and you'll have it." Clarke didn't know his friend James Miller was kidding him, so he went home and did just what Miller suggested and named his music "The Caledonian Hunt's Delight", and it became a popular air for dances and other social festivities. Later Bobbie Burns thought enough of the tune to pen his own stanzes to its meter, "Ye Banks And Braes of Bonnie Doon" and soon the music was being called "Bonnie Doon". Still later, someone else discovered that Wesley's "Wrestling Jacob" could be sung to the music known as "Bonnie Doon" and soon it found its way into the hymnals. And later still, in honor of Methodist Bishop Warren A. Candler, founder and Chancellor of Atlanta's Emory University, who used to sing those words to that tune, the name of the music was changed a third time to "Candler", which in reality is actually "Bonnie Doon" which in turn is "The Caledonian Hunt's Delight"! Let us sing a stanza of this hymn together. (If this tune is not available, let the stanzas be sung to the tune "St. Catherine" — Faith Of Our Fathers — without repeating the last two lines of each stanza.)

———————————————

God took the lyrics of His love and in the midst of days
Gave Charles a thousand tongues to sing his great Redeemer's praise;   .
For half a century he sang in many a metered rhyme
The hymns that Christians will be singing till the end of time.

With quills plucked from an angel's wing, borne earthward by the dove,
He wrote un-numbered stanzas of the Saviour and His love.
His timeless tomes ring through the years wher'er the Church is found,
And when men sing his sacred songs, Aye, that is holy ground!
The history of the Wesleyan movement may be traced by the kinds of hymns Wesley wrote as year gave way to year, and as the fellowship grew and as opposition developed and threatened to destroy the Methodist people, laity as well as clergy. It was in 1749, the very same year that Charles was married to Miss Sarah Gwynne, that the enemies of the new revival began to become more outspoken in their opposition and more active in their persecution. It was that year that saw "the sweet singer of Methodism" pen the militant stanzas of a hymn inspired by the last chapter of Paul's letter to the Ephesians:
Soldiers of Christ, arise, And put your armour on,
Strong in the strength which God supplies Through His eternal Son;
Strong in the Lord of hosts, And in His mighty power,
Who in the strength of Jesus trusts, Is more than conqueror.
Let us sing this stanza to the hymntune "Diademata" which another Englishman, Dr. George J. Elvey, composed for

Matthew Bridges' hymn "Crown Him With Many Crowns" in 1868.

———————————

Because some ministers suffered martyrdom on account of their "enthusiastic faith" between the annual meetings of the British Methodist Conferences, and because others would suffer a similar fate before the next meeting of each scheduled Conference, that same year 1749 saw Wesley writing the hymn with which Methodist Conferences now begin their annual sessions, "And Are We Yet Alive", and the one with which they traditionally close, "And Let Our Bodies Part". (A stanza of each of these hymns may be sung here, both to the same tune if possible, the tune "Dennis" by Lowell Mason, or the tune "Boylston", also by Dr. Mason:

And are we yet alive, And see each other's face?
Glory and praise to Jesus give, For His redeeming grace.
And let our bodies part, To different climes repair;
Inseparably joined in heart, The friends of Jesus are.)

———————————

Charles served as an itinerant preacher until 1756, when he settled down in Bristol, dividing his time thereafter between Bristol and London. Proud to be an ordained Anglican clergyman, he kept his close connection with St. Marylebone Church in London, never severing his relationship with the Anglican communion, even refusing finally to be buried in brother John's burying-ground adjoining what is now the Mother Church of World Methodism, City Road Chapel, London. Confessing that "I have lived and I die in the communion of the Church of England", he was laid to rest in the small graveyard adjacent to his "home Church" St. Marylebone.

During the half a century of his creative life, Charles Wesley wrote more than sixty-five hundred hymns, in nearly every conceivable poetic meter and covering almost the entire range of Christian doctrine and practice. If he needed many stanzas to say what he wanted to say, he did so, and "Jesus The Name High Over All" has twenty-two, while "Come Sinners To The Gospel Feast" has twenty-four. Inspired by

Watts to read back into the Old Testament the fulfillment of the New Testament, Wesley in 1750 wrote "Blow Ye The Trumpet Blow", from Leviticus 25 : 8-13, stanzas that were later sung to the intriguing fuguing tune "Lennox" by the New England composer Lewis Edson, the same music to which "Arise, My Soul Arise" was also sung. (If time permits, the congregation can sing a stanza of each of these hymns to the tune "Lennox", the leader pointing out the connection between the Mosaic "Year of Jubilee" from Leviticus and Wesley's spiritual "Year of Jubilee" which he found in Christ's salvation from sin.)

Blow ye the trumpet, blow! The gladly solemn sound
Let all the nations know, To earth's remotest bound,
The year of Jubilee is come! The year of Jubilee is come!
Return, ye ransomed sinners, home.

Arise, my soul, arise; Shake off thy guilty fears;
The bleeding Sacrifice, In my behalf appears;
Before the throne my Surety stands, Before the throne my
        Surety stands,
My name is written on His hands.

———————————

When Wesley was fifty-five, he wrote another familiar hymn, the theme being suggested by Leviticus 8 :35, "Keep the charge of the Lord that ye die not". This hymn, sung to Lowell Mason's tune "Boylston", composed in 1832, is "A Charge To Keep I Have", which begins with this stanza:

A charge to keep I have, A God to glorify;
A never-dying soul to save, And fit it for the sky.

Wesley's humanity stands out in the closing lines of this hymn, for had he been in better spirits he would never have concluded it on the depressing note: Assured if I my trust betray, I shall forever die. For he was too much of an optimist for that. Had he given it just a moment of extra thought, undoubtedly he would have ended his hymn in this manner:

Help me to watch and pray, And on thyself rely;
Assured if I my trust obey, I'll reign with Him on high.

Nevertheless, be that as it may, let us sing several stanzas of this hymn together. In this hymn as well as in all of his poems, Charles faithfully obeyed the counsel of brother John, who said, "When poetry thus keeps its place as the handmaid of piety, it shall attain, not a poor perishable wreath, but a crown that fadeth not away." He wrote hymns inspired by every book of the Old Testament but three and every one in the New Testament but one, and on every conceivable subject pertinent to the Christian life. While the 1905 edition of the American Methodist Hymnal contained one-hundred-twelve from Charles' fluent pen, the 1935 edition whittled that number almost in half, including only fifty-four, but still they are among the noblest and best in all Christian hymnody, and Wesley continues to vie with Watts for numerical supremacy in the hymnals of the ecumenical Church.

————————

One of his sons, Charles Wesley Junior, composed several good hymn tunes, but it was his grandson, Samuel Sebastian Wesley (1810-1876) who found a permanent place alongside his grandfather in the hymnals of the faith, for he composed the splendid tune "Aurelia" for the hymn "Jerusalem The Golden"; it is to this tune that Christians universally sing "The Church's One Foundation Is Jesus Christ Her Lord". Wesley was so used to speaking in rhymes that his dying words, dictated to his beloved Sarah, contained these moving lines:
In age and feebleness extreme, Who shall a sinful worm redeem?
Jesus, my only joy Thou art; Strength of my failing flesh and heart;
O could I catch a smile from Thee, And drop into eternity!
On Saturday, March 29, 1788, at the age of eighty-one, Charles "caught that smile" and dropped into the arms of the King of Kings, whose praises he had so eloquently sung for half a century. Let us close our Hymn Festival by singing Wesley's hymn "Love Divine", written in 1747, the poet's fortieth year, and as typical of his experience and

convictions as any other he was privileged to write during his long and active life,

Love divine, all loves excelling, Joy of heaven to earth come
           down;
Fix in us Thy humble dwelling, All Thy faithful mercies
           crown!
Jesus, Thou art all compassion, Pure, unbounded love Thou
           art;
Visit us with Thy salvation, Enter every trembling heart.

If time permits, other Wesley hymns may be included in the program, as congregational hymns or as solos, duets, quartets or choral selections: Come, Thou Long Expected Jesus; Ye Servants Of God; Rejoice The Lord Is King; Come, Sinners, To The Gospel Feast; Spirit Of Faith Come Down; Jesus, We Look To Thee; Thou Hidden Source Of Calm Repose; O For A Heart To Praise My God; Gentle Jesus, Meek And Mild; How Can A Sinner Know; and others found in standard or denominational hymnals, to tunes of varying familiarity.

A dramatization of the life and ministry of Charles Wesley in two acts is included in the author's book TEN NEW PLAYS FOR CHURCH AND SCHOOL.

JOHN NEWTON
1725-1807
Growing In Grace

Amazing Grace
How Sweet The Name Of Jesus Sounds
Joy Is A Fruit That Will Not Grow
How Tedious And Tasteless The Hours
Safely Through Another Week
Dear Shepherd Of Thy People, Hear
Glorious Things Of Thee Are Spoken
May The Grace Of Christ Our Saviour

God's grace in His unmerited goodness to us whereby, out of His infinite love, He gives to us the gift of salvation; His grace is that God-like quality which moves God to do for us what we do not deserve, namely, to send His only Son to redeem us from destruction and bestow upon us everlasting life. By faith we respond to God's grace, the result of our response being inner peace. On man's side, Christian grace is man's ability to accept what has already been attained, and then to set forth to achieve that which must be accomplished. It is for that reason that the Big Fisherman wrote in 2 Peter 3:18, "grow in grace and in the knowledge of our Lord and Saviour Jesus Christ". Christians who have been the recipients of God's grace must themselves in gratitude to God continue to grow in Christian grace. A fertile egg placed under a setting hen does one of two things: either it becomes a new baby chick or it rots. One thing is certain, that egg never remains the same. A post placed in the ground will do one of two things: either it will begin to grow and sprout new shoots or it will gradually die and rot away. One thing is certain, that post will never remain the same, that is, unless it happens to be a creosoted post. But God has no use whatsoever for creosoted Christians, those who are what they are and hope to remain as they are all the rest of their days. In the realm of living things, one either grows or dies. Therefore, if Christians are not growing in grace, they are losing grace; if grace is not increasing, it is decreasing. A perfect example of growth in Christian grace is afforded us in the life, the ministry and the great hymns of the English divine, John Newton.

Born in London as the only child of a respectable sea-captain father, John was early dedicated to the ministry by his devout but consumptive mother. By the time he was four, he could recite the Westminister catechism as well as many of the hymns of Isaac Watts by heart. He left home to begin the life of a sailor when he was eleven, and by the time he reached seventeen he had thrown aside every religious principle and abandoned himself to the service of Satan.

Only his love for Mary Catlett, whom he met in 1742 but did not marry until 1750, kept a glow of decency burning within his heart. Once he deserted ship, was caught and brought back in chains like a common felon. When his punishment seemed more than he could bear and he contemplated suicide, only his love for Mary preserved his life. Following his release, he entered upon a life of such wickedness that his friends despaired of his sanity. At one time he dwelt among the cruel slavers of Sierra Leone, and was so mistreated by his Portugese master's Negro wife that he said of himself later, "Had you seen me go so pensive and solitary in the dead of night to wash my one shirt upon the rocks and afterward to put it on wet that it might dry on my back while I slept; had you seen me so poor a figure that when a ship's boat came to the island shame often constrained me to hide myself in the woods from the sight of strangers; had you known that my conduct, principles and heart were still darker than my outward condition — how little would you have imagined that such a one was reserved to be so peculiar an instance of the providential care and exuberant goodness of God. The only good desire I had left was to get back to England to marry Mary."

It was after further humiliation and suffering that Newton boarded a slave-carrying vessel for home, spending some days reading "The Imitation of Christ". His conscience now reawakened, a storm as violent as one nature was wreaking on the wild waves broke over his evil soul, and from that day onward he regarded March 10, 1748 as his "spiritual birthday". It was not until six years later, however, in August, 1754, when he reached Liverpool at the end of another voyage, that he considered himself truly and completely "saved" from his life of sin and degradation. It was of this period in his life that he wrote when he later penned his autobiographical hymn, first published in 1779, in which he sang of God's "grace" no less than six times in twelve lines:

1. Amazing grace — how sweet the sound — That saved a wretch like me!

   I once was lost but now am found, Was blind, but now I see.

2. 'Twas grace that taught my heart to fear, And grace my fears relieved;

   How precious did that grace appear, The hour I first believed!

3. Through many dangers, toils and snares, I have already come;

   'Tis grace has brought me safe thus far, And grace will lead me home.

Let us sing these stanzas to the early American folktune with which they are now associated, remembering that while many who sing may not feel like wretches in their own hearts, the man who penned those words did!

———————————

Six years were to pass between Newton's "spiritual birthday" in 1748 and that memorable day in 1754 when he felt himself a truly regenerated believer, and it was during those years that he learned that "growing in grace" was the way Christians showed their gratitude to God for "the gift of His grace" and his growth continued until the day of his death at the age of eighty-two, December 21, 1807. He appreciated God's grace enough to accept it, and then proceeded to grow in the graces of the Christian life, "grace" undoubtedly meaning to him "the sum total of all Christian virtues". His was no lop-sided life, with one grace being emphasized beyond its relative importance or to the exclusion of others, but a well-rounded, whole, and holy life with every grace being like the circumference of a circle, equidistant from the center, which is Christ Himself. He said of his awakening, "I cried to the Lord with a cry like that of the ravens which yet the Lord does not disdain to hear. And I remembered Jesus whom I had so often derided." As he grew in grace, he grew to love the Name of Him whose Name he had so often used only in foul oaths and evil epithets, and thus he was able to write:

1. How sweet the Name of Jesus sounds, In a believer's ear!

   It soothes his sorrows, heals his wounds, And drives away his fear.

2. Dear Name! the Rock on which I build, My Shield, and Hiding Place,

   My never-failing Treasury, filled With boundless stores of grace.

Let us sing several stanzas of this hymn as we recall the author's growth in grace. (While these lines are sung to several Common Meter tunes, such as "St. Peter", and "Holy Cross", they should be sung to a tune with which the congregation is familiar.)

———————————

As Newton continued to grow in grace, he learned to accept God's gifts of holy joy and heavenly peace. Looking back upon his wicked and barren past, he realized that he had sought for joy in the wrong places with the wrong methods and motives, forgetting that it is a gift of God to those who trust Him and love Him and obey Him. With that in mind he wrote the hymn:

1. Joy is a fruit that will not grow, In nature's barren soil;

   All we can boast till Christ we know, Is vanity and toil.

2. But where the Lord has planted grace, And made His
glories known,
There fruits of heavenly joy and peace, Are found —
and there alone.
Even the Name of Jesus and the mention of holy joy are
inseparable from God's gift of grace, and the poet feels
compelled to link them all together in the stanzas of these
great hymns. Let us sing a stanza or two of this hymn at
this time. (These stanzas may also be sung to any familiar
Common Meter tune, although various different tunes are
used in several different denominational Hymnals.)

— — — — — — — — —

His joy is further illustrated in one of Newton's strangest
and yet one of his most popular hymns, "How Tedious And
Tasteless The Hours":
1. How tedious and tasteless the hours, When Jesus no longer I see!
Sweet prospects, sweet birds and sweet flowers, Have all
lost their sweetness to me;
The midsummer sun shines but dim, The fields strive in
vain to look gay;
But when I am happy in Him, December's as pleasant
as May.
While some people find it difficult to believe that these lovely
words came from the pen of the same convert who told his
story in "Amazing Grace", this is but further proof of the
author's growth in grace as he developed in the Christian
life. These stanzas, too, are sung to an old American camp-
meeting melody. As we sing them, let us remember the heart
out of which they came and the stages of growth they illus-
trate.

— — — — — — — — —

Not only did John Newton learn to love the Name of his
Lord, and to accept and enjoy His blessed gifts of joy and
peace, but he came to respect and honor God's Day as the
holy Sabbath day, and to enjoy serving his Master on the day
that formerly he had wasted in wild revelry. It was in 1774
that he was inspired to pen his majestic Sabbath Day hymn,

and the passing of two centuries has not in any way dimmed its lustre, for it still is one of the noblest Sunday hymns in all hymnody. Set to the tune "Sabbath" by Dr. Lowell Mason in 1824, it is heard week after week throughout all the various branches of Christendom, few knowing that it came from the mind and heart of the same man who exposed his conversion to public view in his hymn "Amazing Grace". Newton's hymn begins with these lines:

1. Safely through another week, God has brought us on our way;

   Let us now a blessing seek, Waiting in His courts today.

   Day of all the week the best, Emblem of eternal rest.

2. While we pray for pardoning grace, Through the dear Redeemer's Name,

   Show Thy reconciled face, Take away our sin and shame;

   From our worldly cares set free, May we rest this day in Thee.

Even in his "Sunday Hymn", Newton continues to praise "God's pardoning grace", as if confessing that apart from that grace, he himself would not be honoring God's day, much less His Name or His Person or His Word!

———————————

As he gradually came to consecrate his entire life to Christ, Newton felt the call to the Christian ministry, to which his deceased mother had so early set him apart. After two miraculous escapes from death, and several years of intense study under John Wesley, George Whitfield and other Churchmen, he was appointed a minister of the Church of England on December 16, 1758. Six years later he went to Olney, where he was ordained a deacon and then a priest. It was here that his intimate fellowship with another poet, William Cowper, began, a friendship that resulted in the publication of their "Olney Hymns" in 1779.

In this remarkable collection of 349 hymns (283 by Newton and 66 by Cowper), the great sacred stanzas of John Newton appeared in print for the first time. It was from this volume that they eventually found their way into the hymnals and hearts of universal Christendom. Incidentally, Hymn

41 of Book 1 is "Amazing Grace". It was that very same year that Newton made his last move, going to London to serve two congregations in Britain's largest city. That historic volume on which Newton and Cowper ("God Moves In A Mysterious Way", "O For A Closer Walk With God" and others) collaborated in 1779 contained another evidence of the author's growth in grace, for it contained the hymns in which he evidenced his love for God's House and his loyalty to God's Kingdom. For God's House he wrote:

1. Dear Shepherd of Thy people, hear; Thy presence now
    display;
    As Thou hast given a place for prayer, So give us hearts
    to pray.
2. Within these walls let holy peace And love and concord
    dwell;
    Here give the troubled conscience ease, The wounded
    spirit heal.
3. The hearing ear, the seeing eye, The humbled mind
    bestow;
    And shine upon us from on high, To make our graces
    grow.

The Church, for Newton, was the place where we learn "to make our graces grow". Let us sing these stanzas together. (Select any Common Meter tune with which the congregation is familiar. If one is not available, let a soloist or quartet or choir interpret the hymn to any suitable tune.)

————————

For God's Kingdom, he wrote these majestic lines, which are sometimes sung to Haydn's "Austrian Hymn", a tune composed in honor of the birthday of Emperor Franz Joseph, but one that has become wedded, in recent decades, to several stirring hymns in the collections of the various denominations:

1. Glorious things of Thee are spoken, Zion, city of our
    God;
    He whose word cannot be broken, Formed thee for His
    own abode;

On the Rock of Ages founded, What can shake thy sure
   repose?
With salvation's wall surrounded, Thou mayst smile at
   all thy foes.
2. See, the streams of living waters, Springing from eternal
   love,
Well supply thy sons and daughters, And all fear of want
   remove;
Who can faint while such a river, Ever flows their thirst
   to assuage;
Grace, which like the Lord the Giver, Never fails from
   age to age.

Here, as in his other superb hymns, Newton cannot sing of
God's Kingdom apart from God's grace.

———————————

This remarkable man continued to preach until his eighti-
eth birthday had passed, and even then he insisted on being
assisted by his old faithful servant to the pulpit of his Church,
St. Mary, Woolnoth, London, so he could read his message
from his manuscript. When advised to give up preaching because of the infirmities of age, the old giant replied, "What!
Shall the old African blasphemer stop while he can speak?"
He even continued his lengthy correspondence with some of
the leading religious and political personages of his day, letters which were later edited and published and widely read
by those who knew, respected and revered the man who had
become the recognized leader of the Evangelical party of
the Anglican Communion, and who, by the excellence of his
original hymns, had revived congregational singing within
the Established Church. The Rev. John Newton even wrote
his own epitaph and added to it this admonition, "I earnest-
ly desire that no other monument and no inscription but to
this purport may be attempted for me". The epitaph contains these words:

"John Newton, Clerk, once an infidel and libertine, was,
by the rich mercy of our Lord and Saviour, JESUS CHRIST,
preserved, restored, pardoned and appointed to preach the

faith he had long labored to destroy, near sixteen years at Olney in Bucks and twenty-eight years in this Church."

Let us close our service by singing the stanzas of another of John Newton's hymns, a benediction in poetry that again emphasizes the principal theme of all of his poems and hymns, God's grace. (These lines may be sung to the tune "Love Divine").

1. May the grace of Christ our Saviour, And the Father's boundless love,
   With the Holy Spirit's favor, Rest upon us from above.
   Thus may we abide in union, With each other and the Lord,
   And possess, in sweet communion, Joys which earth cannot afford. Amen.

REGINALD HEBER
1783-1826
The Church Year

Epiphany: Brightest And Best Of The Sons Of The
        Morning
Trinity Sunday: Holy, Holy, Holy
Communion: Bread Of The World In Mercy Broken
Evening Worship: God That Madest Earth And Heaven
Missionary Sunday: From Greenland's Icy Mountains
St. Stephen's Day: The Son Of God Goes Forth To War
First Sunday After Epiphany: By Cool Siloam's Shady Rill

Reginald Heber, one of England's greatest hymn writers,
was born at Malpas, Cheshire, on April 21, 1783, the second
son of the Rev. Reginald Heber, man of wealth and learning,
and co-rector of the Malpas parish of the Anglican Church.
Reginald's elder brother, Richard, was a book collector who
had accumulated over one-hundred and fifty-thousand volumes. Thus the younger lad had every opportunity which
education and culture could afford. He early displayed his
unusual literary talents, versifying the "Phaedrus" when only
seven years of age. In 1800, at seventeen, he entered Oxford
University and during his first year there won the coveted
Newdigate Prize with a remarkable poem "Palestine" which
was received with such applause as had never before been
heard in that sedate gathering. The original manuscript of
this unusual poem eventually found its way to the National
Library in Madrid and was presented by the Spanish Gov-
ernment to the late Mr. Alexander Weddell of Richmond,
Virginia, in appreciation for his services as the United States
Ambassador to Spain. (This historic document was loaned

to me by Mr. Weddell when he was living in Richmond, some years prior to his accidental death, and it is now among his other papers in his museum-home in the Windsor Farms section of Richmond.)

Following his graduation from Oxford, Reginald spent two years in extensive travel, visiting many European countries before returning to England. Taking Holy Orders and qualifying for the ministry of the Anglican (or Established) Church, he began his work as a clergyman in the village of Hodnet, marrying the daughter of the Dean of the Church there and settling down to a pastorate that was to last for fifteen years.

Early in his ministry, Heber began writing hymns, preparing many of his stanzas for special days in the Anglican Church calendar. In 1811, his twenty-eighth year, the talented pastor jotted down the stanzas of an original Advent poem in a little exercise book in which one of his daughters did her arithmetic lessons, thus giving to Christendom the beautiful Epiphany hymn "Brightest and Best Of The Sons Of The Morning":

1. Brightest and best of the sons of the morning,
   Dawn on our darkness and lend us Thine aid;
   Star of the East, the horizon adorning,
   Guide where our infant Redeemer is laid.

2. Cold on His cradle the dew-drops are shining;
   Low lies His head with the beasts of the stall;
   Angels adore Him in slumber reclining,
   Maker and Monarch and Saviour of all.

3. Say, shall we yield Him in costly devotion,
   Odors of Edom and offerings divine?
   Gems of the mountain and pearls of the ocean,
   Myrrh from the forest and gold from the mine.

4. Vainly we offer each ample oblation;
   Vainly with gifts would His favor secure;
   Richer by far is the heart's adoration;
   Dearer to God are the prayers of the poor.

The author repeated his first stanza as the fifth and last stanza of this beautiful carol-hymn. It was not until eighty-one years later, however, in 1892, that Mr. James P. Harding composed an anthem from which this tune was taken, the hymn tune being appropriately named "Morning Star". It is to this music that Heber's hymn is now universally sung. (A soloist, a small musical group, a full Junior or Adult Choir or the entire congregation may sing several stanzas of this hymn here.)

— — — — — — — — —

The hymn Heber wrote for Trinity Sunday, the Sunday after Pentecost or WhitSunday, is now considered one of the most majestic hymns for Sunday Morning as well as for the Opening of Worship to be found in all hymnody. The first line of his opening stanza is taken directly from Revelation 4:8, "Holy, holy, holy, is the Lord God Almighty", while the other three stanzas abound in the phraseology of the Revelation of St. John:

1. Holy, Holy, Holy, Lord God Almighty, Early in the morning our song shall rise to Thee;
   Holy, Holy, Holy, Merciful and Mighty; God in Three Persons, blessed Trinity!
2. Holy, Holy, Holy, All the saints adore Thee, Casting down their golden crowns around the glassy sea;
   Cherubim and seraphim falling down before Thee, Which wert and art and evermore shalt be.
3. Holy, Holy, Holy, Though the darkness hide Thee, Though the eye of sinful man Thy glory may not see,
   Only Thou art holy; there is none beside Thee, Perfect in power, in love and purity.
4. Holy, Holy, Holy, Lord God Almighty! All Thy works shall praise Thy name in earth and sky and sea;
   Holy, Holy, Holy, Merciful and Mighty! God in Three Persons, blessed Trinity!

The tune to which these lines are now sung was composed by Rev. John Bacchus Dykes, another Anglican divine, in 1861. He named his tune "Nicaea" since it was at the Council of Nicaea in 325 A.D. that the Christian doctrine of the Holy Trinity was fully and finally formulated. (Even though the service may be held one evening, it will be appropriate here to invite the assembled congregation to sing several stanzas of this Trinity Sunday hymn, with a word of explanation that is a Trinity Hymn as well as a Morning Hymn, and therefore may be sung at any appropriate time of the day.)

————————————

On the Friday before Pentecost or WhitSunday (White-Sunday, to be exact, from the custom of wearing white on that day) 1819 when Heber was a maturing pastor of thirty-six, the poet-preacher was visiting in the home of his father-in-law, who was then serving as vicar of Wrexham, an ancient town in North Wales. The older man said to his youthful colleague, "Reginald, on Sunday morning we are to receive in all the Churches the annual offering for 'The Society for the Propagation of the Gospel in Foreign Parts'. — (Incidentally this was the very Society under whose auspices John and Charles Wesley had made their ill-fated missionary visit to America in 1735) — I plan to preach a missionary sermon and then receive the special offering." "What will you take as your text?" the young minister asked. The older man replied, "The Great Commission, of course — 'Go ye into all the world and preach the gospel to every creature'." "Is your sermon complete?" the son-in-law asked. "Except for a good concluding story or poem," the elderly vicar replied. Then, pointing to his gifted visitor, he added, "Reginald, what's the good of having a poet for a son-in-law if he cannot write a poem when his father-in-law needs one?" Young Heber smiled. "A poem? For what occasion?" "For my Sunday morning sermon," Dean Shipley explained. "Seriously, Reginald, try your hand at it. I need some stirring verses with which to conclude my message. See what you can do for me." The young man agreed to try, more to humor his father-in-law than with the thought of writing himself into poetic immortality. He glanced at a globe in the corner of the study, picked up some paper and a pen, sat down in an easy chair at the opposite end of the large room and soon was deeply engrossed in his own thoughts. Half an hour later he looked up from his writing and said, "I have something here, Dean Shipley, if you care to hear it." "By all means, Reginald", the other man replied enthusiastically. "Read what you have written." Heber read slowly and with evident emotion:

1. From Greenland's icy mountains, From India's coral strand;

   Where Afric's sunny fountains, Roll down their golden sand;

   From many an ancient river, From many a palmy plain, They call us to deliver Their land from error's chain.

2. What though the spicy breezes Blow soft o'er Ceylon's isle;

   Though every prospect pleases, And only man is vile;

   In vain with lavish kindness, The gifts of God are strown;

   The heathen in his blindness Bows down to wood and stone.

3. Shall we, whose souls are lighted With wisdom from on high —

   Shall we, to men benighted, The lamp of life deny?

   Salvation! O Salvation! The joyful sound proclaim,

   Till earth's remotest nation Has learned Messiah's Name.

"Majestic, Reginald; superb," the older man exclaimed. "That is precisely what I wanted. Let me have a copy, please." But the younger man hesitated a moment, and said, "The hymn is not complete. It needs a closing stanza of greater majesty." The older man protested, "No, Reginald. Anything else will be anti-climatic. Let the stanzas remain as they are now." But Heber shook his head and said, "No, let me try my hand at another stanza. I think I know just what the poem needs to make it complete." "As you say, Reginald," the other man said, "but I doubt if anything else will improve what you have already written."

While the older man resumed his work on the forthcoming sermon, Heber took up his pen and began writing the fourth and final stanza of the greatest missionary hymn in the English language since Rev. Isaac Watts had published "Jesus Shall Reigh Where'er The Sun" a hundred years earlier, in 1719. After fifteen minutes he called out, "Listen to this." Dean Shipley looked up and listened intently as Heber read:

4. Waft, waft ye winds His story, And you, ye waters, roll,
   Till, like a sea of glory, It spreads from pole to pole;
   Till o'er our ransomed nature, The lamb for sinners slain,

Redeemer, King, Creator, In bliss returns to reign!

"Magnificent, Reginald," Dean Shipley said. "Forgive me for ever questioning your judgment. Those closing lines give the hymn exactly what it needed." The following Sunday morning Dean Shipley read the new poem at the close of his sermon, and then received the special missionary offering. Later it was sung to the tune of a currently popular ballad "Twas When The Seas Were Roaring". While we do not know exactly how much money he received on that occasion, we have it on good authority that the original manuscript of Heber's hymn brought in more money when it was auctioned off to the highest bidder a century after it was written than it originally brought out from the pocket-books of Dean Shipley's congregation.

Five years after "From Greenland's Icy Mountains" was written in England, a friend in England clipped a copy of the poem from a current periodical and mailed it to Miss Mary W. Howard, a member of the Independent Presbyterian Church, Savannah, Georgia. The choir director at this historic Church at that time was Lowell Mason, a young bank clerk who had been employed by the Church as "principal of the singers" as of January 1, 1815, at a salary of one-thousand dollars a year. The twenty-four year old musical-minded business man proved so efficient that on February 2, 1820 he had been elected Church organist as well. Nine years after taking over the congregation's choral responsibilities and four years after being elected Church organist, during the year 1824, Miss Howard, finding no tune to fit Heber's words to her satisfaction, took the clipping to her Church organist, requesting him to do what he could to set them to appropriate music. The musician acceded to her unusual request and, as rapidly as Heber had penned his memorable lines several years earlier and several thousands of miles distant, composed his original tune, naming it fittingly "Missionary Hymn", and dedicating it to Miss Howard. A photographic copy of Mason's original manuscript hangs to this very day on the wall of the reception room in the Educational Building of Independent Presbyterian Church. It was during that same year that Mason composed his splendid tune "Sabbath" for Rev. John Newton's majestic hymn "Safely Through Another Week", and "Hamburg" for Rev. Isaac Watts' hymn "When I Survey The Wondrous Cross", all three of these hymns being sung for the first time that very year by the Choir and congregation of this famous Church. (The Leader may here invite the congregation to sing several stanzas of Heber's missionary hymn, and a stanza or two of the other two hymns as well.)

———————————

From this same period in Reginald Heber's life came the beautiful stanzas of an evening hymn "God That Madest Earth And Heaven", which are sung to the Welsh tune usually associated with the lovely song "All Through The Night";
God that madest earth and heaven, Darkness and light;
Who the day for toil hast given, For rest the night;
May Thine angel-guards defend us, Slumber sweet Thy
          mercy send us;
Holy dreams and hopes attend us, This live-long night.
In 1864 a second stanza was added by William Mercer, and a third stanza later on by Richard Whately, and it is in the form of a three-stanza hymn that this "Evening Song" now appears in most hymnals and songbooks.
(The congregation may be invited to sing these stanzas, or else a soloist may interpret one or two stanzas as the program proceeds.)

———————————

After twice refusing the position as a Missionary Bishop

of his Church, Heber in 1823, four years after writing "From Greenland's Icy Mountains", accepted the call to serve his Lord as Bishop of Calcutta for the Church of England. He announced that "the clergyman should be like the soldier or sailor, bound to go on any service however remote or undesirable, where the course of his duty leads him." His foreign parish was to be an unusually large one: all of India, the island of Ceylon and the whole of Australia. Before he left England, never to return, he wrote a Communion hymn, "Bread Of The World In Mercy Broken" and the familiar lines of "By Cool Siloam's Shady Rill". While Heber's elderly ecclesiastical superior, Archbishop Manners Sutton, refused to sanction the use of these new hymns in the regular services of the Church, he is remembered today only because he did not appreciate or approve of the younger clergyman's original hymns.

1. Bread of the world in mercy broken, Wine of the soul in mercy shed,
   By whom the words of life were spoken, And in whose death our sins are dead.
2. Look on the heart by sorrow broken, Look on the tears by sinners shed;
   And be Thy feast to us the token, That by Thy grace our souls are fed.

This hymn is generally sung to the tune "Eucharistic Hymn" by J. S. B. Hodges (1830-1915) while Isaac B. Woodbury's tune "Siloam" is that to which these lines are sung:

1. By cool Siloam's shady rill, How sweet the lily grows!
   How sweet the breath beneath the hill, Of Sharon's dewy rose!
2. Lo, such the child whose early feet, The paths of peace have trod;
   Whose secret heart, with influence sweet, Is upward drawn to God.
3. O Thou, whose infant feet were found, Within Thy Father's shrine,
   Whose years, with changeless virtue crowned, Were all alike divine:

4. Dependent on Thy bounteous breath, We seek Thy grace
   alone,
   In childhood, manhood, age and death, To keep us still
   Thine own.

— — — — — — — —

The hymn "The Son Of God Goes Forth To War" which Heber penned for St. Stephen's Day, the day after Christmas in the Anglican calendar, is a memorial to Stephen, the first Christian martyr, whose story is told in Acts 7:54-56. In its four stirring stanzas the poet reviews Church history from the days of the twelve Apostles through the martyrdom of Stephen down through the centuries, concluding with reminiscent phrases hinting at the deaths of the forty wrestlers on a frozen lake in Armenia (a noble army, men and boys) as well as the martyrdom of the Two Margarets, the Wigton Martyrs, Margaret Wilson and Margaret McLaughlin, who were drowned at Solway Firth, Scotland, on May 11, 1685 (the matron and the maid):

1. The Son of God goes forth to war, A kingly crown to
   gain;
   His blood-red banner streams afar, Who follows in His
   train?
   Who best can drink his cup of woe, Triumphant over
   pain,
   Who patient bears his cross below, He follows in His
   train!

2. The martyr first, whose eagle eye, Could pierce beyond
   the grave,
   Who saw his Master in the sky, And called on Him to
   save;
   Like Him, with pardon on his tongue, In midst of mortal
   pain,
   He prayed for them that did the wrong, Who follows in
   his train?

Stephen had died like his Lord with a prayer of pardon for his executioners on his lips "in midst of mortal pain."

3. A glorious band, the chosen few, On whom the Spirit
   came,

Twelve valiant saints, their hope they knew, And mocked
the cross and flame;
They met the tyrant's brandished steel, The lion's gory
mane;
They bowed their necks the death to feel: Who follows
in their train?

4. A noble army, men and boys, The matron and the maid,
Around the Saviour's throne rejoice, In robes of light
arrayed:
They climbed the steep ascent of heaven, Through peril,
toil and pain;
O God, to us may grace be given, To follow in their train.

Little did the poet-preacher dream as he wrote these lines
that he too was to "climb the steep ascent of heaven Through
peril, toil and pain". After only three brief years as a Missionary Bishop, when he was forty-three years of age and
reaching the zenith of his powers as a preacher, poet and able
administrator, he died on Monday, April 3, 1826. After a
strenuous Sunday, he retired late only to rise early the next
morning to take a swim in a pool in the yard of the home in
which he was staying in Madras, India. When he plunged
into the seven foot pool, the shock of the cold water against
his hot and weary body caused the bursting of a blood vessel
in the brain. When a servant discovered his body an hour
later, Heber had already gone to give an account of his
stewardship to Him Whom he worshipped as "King of
Kings and Lord of Lords".

Sung to the tune "All Saints, New" which Henry Stephen
Cutler (1824-1902) composed in 1872, this is as challenging
a call to vital Christian discipleship as exists in all hymnic
literature. Composer Cutler pioneered by being one of the
first organists and choir masters in the United States to vest
his singers. He put robes on his boys' choir in the Church of
the Annunciation, New York City, as early as 1852. On
Sunday, October 7, 1860 his vested adult choir made history
and established precedents that abide to this day. However,
while on a month's leave of absence from his post on a concert tour, the Church Vestry dismissed him from their em-

ploy, whereupon Cutler accepted a similar position in another Church in the same city, serving with distinction until his death. He terminated his services at the Church of the Annunciation on June 30, 1865, thus depriving that congregation of the privilege of boasting that Cutler's finest hymn tune had been composed while in their employ!

Heber's widow gathered together many of his hymns and poems and published them in 1827, the year after his untimely death, in a volume entitled "Hymns Written And Adapted To The Weekly Service Of The Year". It was from this post-humous publication that many of his finest works found their way into the hymnals of the Universal Church.

Let us sing in closing the stanzas of Heber's noblest hymn, "The Son Of God Goes Forth To War".

(The complete story of the Wigton Martyrs is found in this author's volume "Dramatized Stories of Hymns and Hymn Writers," pages 230-232; W. A. Wilde Company, Natick, Massachusetts.)

SAMUEL FRANCIS SMITH

1808-1895
Christian Patriotism
My Country Tis Of Thee
Lord Of Our Life
Softly Fades The Twilight Ray
The Morning Light Is Breaking
The Missionary's Farewell

Can a person be both a devout Christian and an ardent patriot? Is there any conflict between one's love of country and one's love of God? Does one love counteract or enrich the other? In Psalm 33:12 we read "Blessed is the nation whose God is the Lord", an admonition to every nation to make God Lord in deed as well as in truth. When Jesus was tempted by a Scribe who asked Him which was the greatest commandment of all, He replied, "Thou shalt love the Lord thy God with all thy heart, with all thy soul, with all thy mind and with all thy strength; and the second is like unto it, thou shalt love thy neighbour as thyself", seeing no apparent conflict between love of God and love of neighbour. In fact Jesus seemed to hint that one could not love one's neighbour rightly unless first of all one loved one's God, nor could one truly love God apart from loving one's neighbour as well, there being a close interaction between the various directions and outreaches of Christian love. A vivid contrast between two types of patriotism is seen when one compares Commodore Stephen Decatur's famous toast, delivered in Norfolk, Virginia in April 1816, "My country; in her intercourse with other nations may she always be in the right; but my country, right or wrong", with the poetic prose of Rev. Francis Bellamy's original Pledge of Allegiance to The American Flag written for Columbus Day celebrations in October, 1892:

"I pledge allegiance to my flag and to the Republic for which it stands; one nation, indivisible, with liberty and justice for all."

Confusion exists sometimes because of a misunderstanding of terms. Love for one's country does not imply hatred for other countries, any more than love for one's race implies hatred for other races. One can love one's native land and remain somewhat neutral toward other lands as one loves one's wife and children while maintaining a neutral attitude toward someone else's family. The impression that one cannot love one land or one family without hating the others is entirely false and erroneous.

We are expected to love our families, our cities, our states, our nations, our churches, our lodges and our love for God only intensifies and strengthens as well as purifies these other lesser loves. This is illustrated with dramatic clarity in the life and ministry of the famous Baptist clergyman, Rev. Samuel Francis Smith. This remarkable man was born in Boston, Massachusetts, October 21, 1808. Following his graduation from Harvard University in 1829 at the age of twenty-one, he entered Andover Theological Seminary to prepare himself for the Christian ministry. On the memorable afternoon of Februrary 2, 1832, just a few months after he had celebrated his twenty-third birthday, the young student went up to his room at 147 Main Street, Andover, Massachusetts, to go over some German papers, manuscripts and documents which the hymnologist from Boston, Lowell Mason, had entrusted to his care. Mason's friend, William Channing Woodbridge, had made a trip to Britain and the continent of Europe investigating and studying the use of music in the public schools there, gathering a great deal of materials enroute. Mason, knowing of Smith's proficiency in translating German, had left many of Woodbridge's papers with him, requesting the young student to sort out what he considered worthwhile, translate into usable English what he thought could be of use in American schools, and generally give Woodbridge's materials a thorough going-over. That afternoon Smith came across the words of a patriotic song and the melodic line of a simple melody to which the lines had been sung by some German children in a patriotic public ceremony. He went over the German poem in his mind, and suddenly felt an inner urge to try his own hand at writing a poem in the same mood to match the same tune which Woodbridge had heard in Germany, little dreaming that it was the music to which the British were already singing their national anthem, "God Save The King," a tune attributed to Henry Carey. With almost effortless ease, the words began to become lines and the lines stanzas, and before he put his pen down he had written four original patriotic stanzas that would enshrine him forever in the hearts of his countrymen:

1. My country, tis of thee, Sweet land of liberty, Of thee I sing;
   Land where my fathers died, Land of the pilgrim's pride, From every mountain side, Let freedom ring!

2. My native country, thee, Land of the noble, free, Thy name I love;
   I love thy rocks and rills, Thy woods and templed hills; My heart with rapture thrills, Like that above.

3. Let music swell the breeze, And ring from all the trees, Sweet freedom's song;
   Let mortal tongues awake; Let all that breathe partake; Let rocks their silence break, The sound prolong.

4. Our fathers' God, to thee, Author of liberty, To thee we sing;
   Long may our land be bright, With freedom's holy light; Protect us by thy might, Great God, our King.

Five months later, on July 4, 1832, the Junior Choir of Boston's historic Park Street Church sang this new hymn under the direction of the organist and choir master of the congregation, none other than Dr. Lowell Mason himself. It is not without tremendous significance that our nation's noblest patriotic poem and her finest bit of patriotic prose,

The Pledge to the Flag, came from the pen of Baptist clergymen. Let us sing together the first and fourth stanzas of "America".

———————————

The intensity of Smith's personal devotion to his Lord, to whose ministry he had been called, is seen in a hymn of confession and consecration which he was inspired to write after many years in the active service of the King of Kings, "Lord Of Our Life", dated November, 1891. One senses no conflict whatsoever in the heart of the man who was so ardently patriotic that he could write such a stirring national hymn, and yet so personally devout that he could pen a hymn of this nature. In fact one is almost led to believe that Smith's love for his country was enriched and deepened by his love for God:

1. Lord of our life, God whom we fear, Unknown yet known, unseen yet near;
   Breath of our breath, in thee we live, Life of our life our praise receive.
2. Thine eye detects the sparrow's fall; Thy heart of love expands for all;
   Our throbbing life is full of thee; Throned in thy vast infinity.
3. Shine in our darkness, Light of light, Our minds illume, disperse our night;
   Make us responsive to thy will: Our souls with all thy fulness fill.
4. We love thy name, we heed thy rod; Thy word our law, O gracious God;
   We wait thy will; on thee we call; Our light, our life, our love, our all.

This hymn can be sung to any standard Long Meter tune, although it is generally sung to the tune "Louvan" composed by Virgil Taylor in 1846. Let us sing together several stanzas of this devotional hymn.

———————————

Not only was Samuel Francis Smith ardently patriotic and intensely devoted to his Lord, he was also faithfully obedient to God's will and God's law. As a student of the Holy Bible, he familiarized himself with his King's commands and to obey them became not his duty but his delight. In this spirit he observed the first day of the week as God's holy day, the Lord's day, or the Christians' true Sabbath day. To him this day was always a day of joy and peace, symbolic of the joy and peace that would be every believer's possession in God's eternal Kingdom beyond the skies. The very same year that saw him penning his finest patriotic hymn, 1832, saw him also writing the three stanzas of the loveliest Sunday evening hymn in all Christian literature:

1. Softly fades the twilight ray, Of the holy Sabbath day; Gently as life's setting sun, When the Christian's course is run.

2. Peace is on the world abroad, Tis the holy peace of God; Symbol of the peace within, When the spirit rests from sin.

3. Saviour, may our Sabbaths be Days of joy and peace in Thee,
   Till in heaven our souls repose, Where the Sabbath ne'er shall close.

This hymn is generally sung to the lovely tune "Holley" which George Hews composed in 1835 for another evening hymn "Softly Now The Light Of Day". Let us sing this hymn to this tune, remembering that it came from the heart and mind of a man who was aggressively patriotic, intensely committed to the service of his Lord, and faithfully obedient to the Master's commands.

— — — — — — — — —

Finally, Samuel Francis Smith was marvelously and broadly world-minded. He knew that the Gospel of God's Kingdom was never to be the private possession of any nation or denomination, and he had little patience with those who sought to limit God theologically or geographically. When he heard of the work of the pioneer missionary in Burma, Adoniram Judson, he was thrilled and under the spell of those dramatic reports he was inspired to write the first great missionary hymn ever penned on American soil, "The

Morning Light Is Breaking". Watts had written "Jesus Shall Reign" in 1719 and Heber had given Christendom "From Greenland's Icy Mountains" in 1819, but it remained for this young student for the Baptist ministry to write America's first missionary hymn in 1832, the same year in which he wrote his noble patriotic hymn and his surpassingly beautiful Sunday evening hymn:

1. The morning light is breaking, The darkness disappears;
   The sons of earth are waking, To penitential tears;
   Each breeze that sweeps the ocean, Brings tidings from afar
   Of nations in commotion, Prepared for Zion's war.
2. See heathen nations bending, Before the God we love,
   And thousand hearts ascending, In gratitude above;
   While sinners now confessing, The gospel call obey,
   And seek the Saviour's blessing, A nation in a day.
3. Blest river of salvation, Pursue thine onward way;
   Flow thou to every nation, Nor in thy richness stay;
   Stay not till all the lowly Triumphant reach their home;
   Stay not till all the holy Proclaim "The Lord is come!"

While the poet-preacher never became a "foreign missionary", his son, Rev. Dr. A. W. Smith, did give himself to overseas Christian service, proclaiming the good news of the Gospel within the shadow of the "old Moulmein Pagoda" immortalized by Rudyard Kipling in "On The Road To Mandalay". As sung to the tune "Webb" which is the music to which "Stand Up For Jesus" is almost universally sung, although originally composed for a popular song "Tis Dawn, The Lark Is Singing", this missionary hymn still instructs and inspires believers in the message and meaning of The Great Commission. .

————————————

Care and good judgment must be exercised in the selection of hymns for services of public worship, even in the case of such famous missionary hymns as "The Morning Light Is Breaking". On one occasion a Presbyterian ministerial colleague of mine invited a returned missionary to speak to his usual small mid-week prayer-meeting congregation. The host pastor urged his visitor to limit his remarks to twenty or thirty minutes at the most, but when the guest speaker saw the large Wednesday night group that had been "drummed up" by the home pastor, he found it difficult to limit himself, and proceeded to speak for an hour and a half. When he finally said "Amen" and sat down, the presiding clergyman glanced at his order of service and calmly announced, "We will conclude our service by singing Rev. Samuel Francis Smith's well-known missionary hymn, Number so-and-so in our Hymnal." When the sleepy-eyed worshippers found the place at last, and noted that they were about to sing "The Morning Light Is Breaking, The Darkness Disappears," they broke out into hilarious and prolonged laughter, saying out loud to one another, "Isn't it so! Isn't it so!" The pastor could do nothing then but pronounce the benediction and go home.

His feeling for those early missionaries moved Smith to write another hymn which became quite popular during the first half of the nineteenth century, a rather tragic bit of heart-rending poetry entitled "The Missionary's Farewell". It was sung publicly for the first time at a farewell meeting held in Philadelphia on May 18, 1833, when Rev. and Mrs. Matthew Laird and Rev. and Mrs. John Cloud were preparing to follow Rev. John Pinney, the pioneer Presbyterian missionary, to Monrovia, Liberia, and was used again on May 29, 1833 when Rev. and Mrs. William Reed and Rev. and Mrs. John C. Lowrie prepared to depart from the same city for missionary work in India:

1. Yes, my native land, I love thee, All thy scenes I love them well;
   Friends, connections, happy country, Can I bid you all farewell?
   Can I leave you, Far in heathen lands to dwell?

2. Home, thy joys are passing lovely; Joys no stranger heart can tell;
   Happy home, tis sure I love thee, Can I, can I say farewell?
   Can I leave thee, Far in heathen lands to dwell?

3. Scenes of sacred peace and pleasure, Holy days and
   Sabbath bell;
   Richest, brightest, sweetest treasure, Can I bid you all
   farewell?
   Can I leave you, Far in heathen lands to dwell?
4. Yes, I hasten from you gladly, From the scenes I loved
   so well.
   Far away, ye billows, bear me, Lovely native land, farewell.
   Pleased I leave thee, Far in heathen lands to dwell.
5. In the deserts let me labor, On the mountains let me tell
   How He died, the blessed Saviour, To redeem a world
   from hell.
   Let me hasten, Far in heathen lands to dwell.
6. Bear me on thou restless ocean, Let the winds my canvass
   swell —
   Heaves my heart with warm emotion, While I go far
   hence to dwell.
   Glad I leave thee, Native land, farewell, Farewell.

When, within a few months after arriving in Africa, Rev.
and Mrs. Matthew Laird and Rev. John Cloud died, and
when, shortly after reaching India on October 15, 1833,
Rev. and Mrs. John C. Lowrie and Rev. William Reed
passed away, those who had attended their farewell services
and had sung this hymn recalled its poignant lines and repeated them over and over again, in that way calling to mind
the heroic sacrifices of those first foreign missionaries who
had so gladly and willingly given up their lives for the sake
of the Gospel of Jesus Christ. These moving lines were sung
to many different tunes during the half-century after their
composition, and they may still be found in numbers of old
hymnals. Sometimes they are sung to the tune "Greenville",
an adaptation of an old folk tune, "Go Tell Aunt Nancy, The
Old Gray Goose Is Dead", which necessitates the repetition
of the first phrase of the last line of each stanza. But they
reveal as much of the heart and concern of the poet as they
do of the heroism of those early missionary pioneers "of
whom the world was not worthy".

(A Soloist may sing several of these stanzas here to some appropriate tune). So the hymns of this Baptist clergyman, who died at the age of eighty-seven at his home at 1811 Center Street, Newton, Massachusetts, in 1895, are living illustrations of the fact that every Christian should be ardently patriotic, passionately devoted to his Lord, faithfully obedient to God's commands, and broadly world-minded in his Christian outreach and concern. Let us conclude our service by singing all of the stanzas of Smith's missionary hymn, "The Morning Light Is Breaking".

FANNY CROSBY
1820-1915
Blessed Assurance

Pass Me Not, O Gentle Saviour
Safe In The Arms Of Jesus
Jesus, Keep Me Near The Cross
Rescue The Perishing
Blessed Assurance
Open The Gates Of The Temple
Draw Me Nearer
He Hideth My Soul
Close To Thee
Saviour, More Than Life To Me
Though Your Sins Be As Scarlet
Jesus Is Tenderly Calling
All The Way My Saviour Leads Me
Saved By Grace

The greatest hymn writer in the history of the Christian Church was the co-founder of the Methodist Church, the British divine Rev. Charles Wesley. It is significant that the most successful as well as the most prolific author of gospel hymns and songs was the American Methodist, blind Fanny Crosby. Wesley's life spanned almost the entire length of the eighteenth century, while Fanny Crosby's ninety-five years covered four-fifths of the nineteenth century as well as the first fifteen years of the twentieth. This remarkable woman was born in Southeast, Putnam County, New York, on March 24, 1820. When she was a tiny baby just six weeks old she was permanently blinded when an illiterate housemaid applied hot poultices to her inflamed eyes. When Frances

Jane, for that was the name under which she was baptized, was hardly twelve months old, her father, John Crosby, passed away quite suddenly, leaving the rearing and training of the precocious baby girl to her mother and grandmother. When Frances was nine years of age, the family moved to Ridgefield, Connecticut, where they spent "six beautiful years".

At fifteen she entered the Institution for the Blind in New York City, remaining there as a pupil for twelve years and as an Instructor for many years after graduation. During those formative years as a student, Frances Jane Crosby revealed a truly remarkable talent for making verses and writing poems. Soon she was memorializing many events of public interest in poetic form, and before long her lengthy paeans of praise were being printed in the New York City newspapers while composers began to seek her out to write librettoes and stanzas which they could set to lilting music. George F. Root, who became the most successful and popular author and composer of Civil War Songs, heard of Miss Crosby when he was serving as the organist of New York's "The Church of the Strangers" on Mercer Street and conducting classes for ministeriial students in the city's Union Theological Seminary and he prevailed upon her to write the libretto for his first big musical success "The Flower Queen", published initially in 1852, the poet's thirty-second year. It was while she was teaching at this famous Institution that Miss Crosby became a close friend of the Secretary, Mr. Grover Cleveland, the gifted man who was later to serve two terms as President of the United States. In 1858, Miss Crosby married blind Mr. Alexander Van Alstyne, an accomplished scholar and musician who was also on the faculty of the Institution for the Blind, and their married life was a very happy one, broken only by his death in 1902. While she had been making quite a name for herself as a poet and versifyer for nearly three decades, it was not until she was forty-four years of age that she wrote her first sacred song. Little did she dream when Mr. William Bradbury, (the composer of the tunes for such well-known gospel hymns as "He Leadeth

Me", "Jesus Loves Me", "Sweet Hour Of Prayer", "Just As I Am Without One Plea" and others) approached her on February 5, 1864 with a request that she write appropriate stanzas for a new tune he had just recently composed, that before her death in 1915 she would be privileged to write more than eight thousand hymns and gospel songs. The words she wrote for Bradbury's tune were these:

We are going, we are going, To a home beyond the skies,
Where the fields are robed in beauty, And the sunlight never
    dies;
Where the fount of life is flowing, In the valley green and
    fair,
We shall dwell in love together, There will be no parting
    there.

It was four years later that an Ohio business-man, song leader and composer, Mr. William H. Doane, approached Mrs. Van Alstyne with a request similar to that of Mr. Bradbury's. He had composed a tune and he wanted someone to give it words. Undaunted, the poet accepted his challenge and wrote her first popular gospel song, which began with this stanza and chorus:

    Pass me not, O gentle Saviour, Hear my humble cry;
    While on others Thou art calling, Do not pass me by.
    Saviour, Saviour, hear my humble cry;
    While on others Thou art calling, Do not pass me by.

Although these words have been criticized on the grounds that Christ never passes anyone by — they pass Him by instead — the song continues to be sung by Christians the world over, and has not lost any of its popularity as it approaches its one-hundredth birthday. Let us sing together several stanzas of Fanny Crosby's first popular gospel hymn, "Pass Me Not, O Gentle Saviour".

— — — — — — — —

Later that very same year, 1868, Mr. Doane, a successful Ohio industrialist whose hobby was composing music and directing singing, was again in New York City, and was once more a composer in search of a poet. He rushed to the Van Alstyne home and said to the poet, "I have just forty-five minutes before I have to catch a train for Cincinnati, and I want to play for you a new tune I have just composed. Listen to it and then write some appropriate stanzas, because I'd like to introduce the new song at a Sunday School convention in my home state next month." With that, he went to the piano, played a rousing, stirring tune, and asked his hostess to "set it to words". As he played his music over again several times at her request, she carefully wrote down the words and lines that began to flow through her heart and mind. Thirty minutes later as he picked up his hat and said "Goodbye" she handed him a piece of paper which he put in his pocket as he hurried to make his train. Enroute to Cincinnati that afternoon, Mr. Doane opened the piece of paper and read the stanzas she had written to fit his moving music:

Safe in the arms of Jesus, Safe on His gentle breast,
There by His love o'er shaded, Sweetly my soul shall rest.
Hark, 'tis the voice of angels, Borne on a song to me,
Over the hills of glory, Over the jasper sea.

Safe in the arms of Jesus, Safe on His gentle breast,
There by His love o'er shaded, Sweetly my soul shall rest.

Although this song has, unfortunately, been taken over by the morticians or relegated to funeral parlors in recent years, and is currently sung so dolefully that one gets the erroneous impression that to be "safe in the arms of Jesus" is about as unfortunate a thing as could happen to any self-respecting Christian, let us remember as we sing it together now that it was first sung by several thousand Sunday School scholars at a State Convention, with all the enthusiasm and gusto they could muster for that occasion. Let us sing together "Safe In The Arms Of Jesus".

(When this author's parents met Fanny Crosby at Round Lake, New York, a Methodist Summer Assembly ground, while on their honeymoon in July, 1909, the poet told my father that "Safe In The Arms Of Jesus" was her personal favorite, so my father sang it for her on several occasions both in English and in his native Armenian tongue.)

— — — — — — — —

The followiing year, 1869, Fanny Crosby again collaborated with Mr. Doane on another beautiful gospel hymn which became world-famous:
Jesus, keep me near the cross, There a precious fountain
Free to all, a healing stream, Flows from Calvary's mountain.
In the cross, In the cross, Be my glory ever,
Till my raptured soul shall find, Rest beyond the river.
Let us sing together two stanzas of this familiar gospel song.

— — — — — — — — —

When Fanny Crosby visited New York's "Bowery Mission" in 1880, her sixtieth year, she was already well-known as the author of such best-sellers as "The Blind Girl and Other Poems", published in 1844, "Monteresy and Other Poems", 1849, and "A Wreath of Columbia's Flowers", 1858, while her fame as a sacred poet had made her influence for righteousness even more widespread by means of her hymns and songs. That memorable night, Rev. Albert G. Ruliffson, the founder of the Mission and the President of its first Board of Trustees (and this author's maternal great grandfather) was presiding, and in the course of the service he invited his distinguished guest to say a few words, an invitation she readily accepted. As she went home that night, Fanny Crosby and her companion, the candy manufacturer, Mr. Huyler, talked about the work of the Mission. Later the poet wrote that when Mr. Huyler said, "Isn't it wonderful the work that these rescue missions are doing", she could hardly wait to get home, take off her wraps and write down these lines:
Rescue the perishing, care for the dying, Snatch them in pity
       from sin and the grave;
Weep o'er the erring one, lift up the fallen, Tell them of
      Jesus, the mighty to save.
Rescue the perishing, Care for the dying, Jesus is merciful,
      Jesus will save.
This time she had the privilege of sending her stanzas to Mr. Doane first, and when he set them to music, they immediately sang their way around the Christian world.
Let us sing together, "Rescue The Perishing".

— — — — — — — — —

The first poem Fanny Crosby wrote was penned when she was just nine years of age. She had asked God to use her despite her physical infirmity, and when she felt He had heard her plea and answered it affirmatively, she went to her room and wrote these beautiful lines:

O what a happy soul am I, Although I cannot see;
I am resolved that in this world, Contented I will be.
How many blessings I enjoy, That other people don't;
To weep and sigh because I'm blind, I cannot and I won't!

Little wonder, then, that God could make use of such a spirit. It was in 1873, the poet's fifty-third year, that another dear friend paid her a visit, Mrs. Joseph F. Knapp, the wife of the founder and first president of the Metropolitan Life Insurance Company. While Fanny Crosby held her membership in the Thirtieth Street Methodist Church in New York, the Knapps were active members of the St. John's Methodist Church in the same city. The daughter of a prominent evangelist, Dr. Walter Palmer and his wife, Mrs. Knapp, familiarly known just as Phoebe, had been born in New York City in 1839. Her early training had developed her remarkable musical talents, and soon she was composing as well as playing music. She came to visit her long-time friend that afternoon with a request similar to that of Mr. Bradbury nine years earlier, and it came as no surprise when she said to her hostess, as she sat down at the nearby piano, "Aunt Fanny, I have composed a piece of music and I want you to write words for it". As she played her original tune, the poet's mind recalled the text of the previous Sunday morning sermon, Hebrews 10:22 "Let us draw near with a true heart in full assurance of faith", and almost before she knew it, she was matching Phoebe's tune with these lines:

Blessed assurance, Jesus is mine; Oh what a foretaste of
        glory divine;
Heir of salvation, purchase of love; Born of His spirit,
        washed in His blood.
This is my story, this is my song, Praising my Saviour all the
        day long.

And thus was born one of Fanny Crosby's finest gospel

hymns. It was so typical of her own personal religious faith, that were anyone ever to write a full and definitive biography of this remarkable woman, undoubtedly it should be entitled simply "Blessed Assurance". Let us sing this hymn together.

— — — — — — — —

Later these two friends collaborated on another song, one that has become one of our favorite Palm Sunday and Easter hymns, solos and sacred anthems, "Open The Gates Of The Temple". (The Choir or a Soloist may sing this here.)

— — — — — — — —

The blind poet said on one occasion,
"I think that life is not too long, and therefore I determine That many people hear a song who will not hear a sermon". Yet her songs are sermons in themselves, for they were born in an atmosphere of Christian faith and hope and love and convey that message to everyone who sings or hears them. In 1875 she and Mr. Doane again got together on another hymn that was to prove eminently successful, the consecration hymn, "Draw Me Nearer", which begins with this stanza:
I am Thine O Lord, I have heard Thy voice And it told Thy
        love to me;
But I long to rise in the arms of faith, And be closer drawn
        to Thee.
Draw me nearer, nearer blessed Lord, To the cross where
        Thou hast died;
Draw me nearer, nearer, nearer blessed Lord, To Thy
        precious bleeding side.
So strong and virile was her own faith that she said to a friend one day, "If I were to re-write Tennyson's 'Crossing The Bar' I would not close with the words 'I *hope* to see my Pilot face to face', but rather I would say, 'I *know* I'll see my Pilot face to face, When I have crossed the bar.'" Let us sing together this noble hymn of consecration.

— — — — — — — —

Another of her favorites, "He Hideth My Soul In The Cleft Of The Rock", was set to music by William J. Kirkpatrick. Here let a soloist or quartet sing a stanza or two of this familiar gospel song.

— — — — — — — —

One of her popular "prayer hymns" was set to music by a native New Yorker, Silas J. Vail, in 1874, the simple melody and harmonies of the tune being fittingly adapted to the equally plain but clear affirmations of the poem, which begins:
Thou my everlasting portion, More than friend or life to me,
All along my pilgrim journey, Saviour, let me walk with
    Thee.
Close to Thee, Close to Thee, Close to Thee, Close to Thee,
All along my pilgrim journey, Saviour, let me walk with Thee.
Let us sing a stanza of this devotional hymn together.

———————————

It was in 1875, the year in which they gave us "Draw Me Nearer", that the same poet and same composer again collaborated successfully on "Saviour, More Than Life To Me", a hymn that bears a striking resemblance to the one we have just been singing:
Saviour, more than life to me, I am clinging, clinging close
    to Thee;
Let Thy precious blood applied, Keep me ever, ever near
    Thy side.
Every day, every hour, Let me feel Thy cleansing power;
May Thy tender love to me, Bind me closer, closer, Lord to
    Thee.
Let us sing this first stanza together.

———————————

Mr. Doane later composed a tune for Fanny Crosby's poem, "Though Your Sins Be As Scarlet, They Shall Be As White As Snow", inspired by Isaiah 1:18. Here let a soloist or quartet sing a stanza of this familiar gospel song.

———————————

It was George Coles Stebbins who composed the tune for one of the poet's most effective invitation hymns, "Jesus Is Tenderly Call Thee Home", while a Baptist clergyman, Rev. Robert Lowry, composed the lilting strains of music for another of her fine poems, "All The Way My Saviour Leads Me". Let us sing one stanza of each of these familiar songs:
Jesus is tenderly calling Thee home, Calling today, Calling
    today;

Why from the sunshine of love wilt thou roam, Farther and
        farther away?
Calling today, Calling today, Jesus is calling, is tenderly call-
        ing today.

All the way my Saviour leads me, What have I to ask beside?
Can I doubt His tender mercy, Who through life has been
        my guide?
Heavenly peace, divinest comfort, Here by faith with Him
        to dwell;
For I know whate'er befall me, Jesus doeth all things well.

— — — — — — — —

Some of her best hymns were written "backwards", in that
the music was composed before the words, while others were
written "forwards", the stanzas preceding the music. But
either way, she poured all of her faith into every line of
every stanza. Following her husband's death, she wrote a
stanza that was not discovered until she had gone to join him
in heaven:

'Tis only a leaf, a withered leaf, But its story is fraught with
        pain;
'Twas the gift of one who is far away, And will never return
        again.
He will never return, but I feel ere long, My spirit with his
        will be,
And the old time love shall be sweeter there, Where I know
        he waits for me.

One of her most impressive poems was inspired jointly by
a prayer-meeting talk delivered by Dr. Howard Crosby one
Wednesday night on the subject "Grace", from the text "Yea
though I walk through the valley of the shadow of death, I
will fear no evil", and the minister's own sudden death before the end of that very same week in 1891. As the poet
meditated upon that verse, she suddenly asked herself what
would be her first impression when she entered heaven.
Thinking of her blindness she said, "Why, my eyes will be
opened and I will see my Saviour face to face." When her
friend and publisher Mr. L. H. Bigelow suggested that she

write a hymn on "Grace" sometime later, she wrote out, in less than an hour's time, the stanzas of "Saved by Grace", which began:

Someday the silver cord will break, And I no more as now
      shall sing;
But, oh, the joy when I shall wake, Within the palace of the
      King.
And I shall see Him face to face, And tell the story — saved
      by grace.

She hid the poem away for three years, and revealed it only when she was invited by Mr. Ira D. Sankey, the world-renowned evangelist of sacred song, to speak to a group assembled at one of the Northfield, Massachusetts, summer conferences. After a few brief remarks, she recited her new stanzas. A reporter for a London newspaper wrote them down, took them back with him when he crossed the Atlantic and they appeared in print for the first time in a British paper. When Mr. Sankey discovered them there, he asked George Stebbins to compose an appropriate tune. Stebbins then proceeded to write the music to which these lines are now universally sung. Before we sing this gospel hymn in closing, let me read brief extracts from two more of Fanny Crosby's writings. The first was penned just a few weeks before the author's death at the age of ninety-five, in February, 1915, and bears a striking resemblance to her very first poem, written over half a century earlier:

You will reach the river brink, Some sweet day, bye and bye;
You will find your broken link, Some sweet day, bye and bye.
O the loved ones waiting there, By the tree of life so fair
Till you come their joy to share, Some sweet day, bye and bye.

The other is the closing stanza of a long poetic tribute paid Miss Crosby by her English counter-part, hymn-writer Frances Ridley Havergal, who wrote these lines in 1872:

Dear blind sister over the sea, An English heart goes forth
      to thee.
We are linked by a cable of faith and song, Flashing bright
      sympathy all along;

One in the East and one in the West, Singing for Him whom
     our souls love best,
"Singing for Jesus", telling His love, All the way to our home
     above,
Where the severing sea with its restless tide, Never shall
     hinder and never divide.
Sister! What shall our meeting be, When our hearts shall
     sing and our eyes shall see!

Remember, Fanny Crosby, who continued to write and publish her hymns and songs under her maiden name at her husband's insistence, signed a contract to provide one publisher
with three hymns a week, a contract she faithfully filled for at
least fifty years, in addition to penning hundreds of poems on
miscellaneous subjects and hundreds of hyms and songs for
other composers, musicians, singers and publishers, her total
output surpassing eight-thousand original poems. God had
closed the eyes of her body, she often confessed, in order to
open the eyes of her soul. Little wonder then that her writings mirror the miracle of God's grace. With that in mind, let
us sing together as we conclude our Hymn Festival, Fanny
Crosby's hymn "Saved By Grace". (If time permits, some
other familiar Fanny Crosby songs may be sung as congregational hymns, solos, duets, quartets or Choir selections: Tell
Me The Story Of Jesus (set to music by John Sweney);
Conquering Now And Still To Conquer (also set to music by
Mr. Sweney); Praise Him, Praise Him, Jesus Our Blessed
Redeemer (to Chester Allen's stirring tune), and others.
One or two of these may be substituted in place of some
mentioned in the program, if desirable.

     Further detailed information about Fanny Crosby, her
hymns and songs, and her close connection with two generations of this writer's own family may be found in various
chapters in this author's books: LIVING STORIES OF
FAMOUS HYMNS, 1955, (fifty true stories), FAMOUS
STORIES OF INSPIRING HYMNS, 1956, (fifty more)
and FORTY TRUE STORIES OF FAMOUS GOSPEL
SONGS, 1959, all publications of W. A. Wilde Co., Natick,
Mass.)

A MISSIONARY HYMN FESTIVAL

Jesus Shall Reign
From Greenland's Icy Mountains
The Morning Light Is Breaking
O Zion Haste
Heralds Of Christ
From All The Dark Places
Christ For The World We Sing
Hail To The Brightness Of Zion's Glad Morning
We've A Story To Tell To The Nations
Watchman, Tell Us Of The Night

The first great missionary hymn of modern times was Rev.
Isaac Watts' "Jesus Shall Reign Were'er The Sun", inspired by Psalm 72 and first published in the poet's monumental volume "The Psalms Of David Imitated in the
Language of the New Testament" in 1719. The story of
Watts and this particular hymn is included in the chapter on
ISAAC WATTS: SINGING A NEW SONG elsewhere
in this volume. Here the leader may read aloud Psalm 72,
and then invite the congregation to sing several stanzas of
this hymn to the familiar tune "Duke Street".

Seventy years after the initial publication of Watts' finest
work, a Presbyterian preacher, Rev. Adam Rankin, rode
horseback from his home in Kentucky to the site of the meeting of the First General Assembly of The Presbyterian
Church in the new Republic in the Second Presbyterian
Church of Philadelphia, in May, 1789, for the primary
purpose of pleading with his ministerial brethren "to refuse
to allow the great and pernicious error of adopting the use
of Isaac Watts' hymns in public worship in preference to

Rouse's versifications of the Psalms of David". The Assembly heard him out, and then requested him to "exercise Christian charity with those who differ from him in their views", adding the suggestion thereto that he be "guarded against disturbing the peace of the Church on this matter". Today one would be as hard pressed to forbid the use of these superb hymns as Rankin was in his desire to prohibit their use altogether.

———————————

The second great missionary hymn of modern times was written exactly one-hundred years after Dr. Watts published his famous volume, and was penned by another Anglican divine, Bishop-to-be Reginald Heber, in 1819. The story of the writing of this hymn and the composing of its tune is told in the chapter on REGINALD HEBER: THE CHURCH CALENDAR, elsewhere in this volume. The congregation may then be invited to sing several stanzas of the hymn "From Greenland's Icy Mountains" here.

———————————

The third great missionary hymn of modern times, and the first one to be written by an American on American soil, was twenty-three year old Rev. Samuel Francis Smith's "The Morning Light Is Breaking", penned in 1832, and sung to the stirring tune "Webb". The story of this hymn and tune will be found in the chapter: SAMUEL FRANCIS SMITH: CHRISTIAN PATRIOTISM, elsewhere in this volume. The congregation may then sing several stanzas of this famous hymn.

———————————

The second most popular native American missionary hymn, and the first successful missionary hymn ever written by a woman, was written by London-born Mrs. Mary Ann Thomson in Philadelphia, Pennsylvania, in 1868. The thirty-four year old wife of James Thomson, the librarian of the Free Library of that city, and herself an active member in the Church of the Annunciation, was inspired to write her memorable lines one afternoon when she was trying to quiet and comfort her daughter who was sick with typhoid fever.

Together they had visited, quoted familiar passages of Scripture and then prayed for all sick people the world over, after which the mother had gone to the piano in the next room to play softly several hymn tunes in order to lull her little girl to sleep. Among the tunes she played that afternoon was one of her favorites, the tune "Pilgrims" which the blind composer from Lancashire, England, Henry Smart, had composed earlier that same year for Frederick Faber's hymn "Hark, Hark My Soul! Angelic Songs are Swelling" which had been written fourteen years earlier. Mrs. Thomson had loved this tune the very first time she had heard it and had often hummed its melody and sung its brief Refrain:

Angels of Jesus, Angels of light, Singing to welcome the
    pilgrims of the night.

That particular afternoon, in the light of her conversation with her little girl, and under the spell of Smart's moving music, she felt inspired to write some original stanzas of her own to match the meter of Faber's lines, so they, too, could be sung to the music which she held in such high regard. Soon she was substituting her own words for those of Faber's familiar Refrain, and was singing to Smart's music:

Publish glad tidings, tidings of peace, Tidings of Jesus, re-
    demption and release.

Then, before the afternoon waned, she wrote down six stanzas of her own, in alternating lines of eleven and ten syllables each, so she could sing them to Smart's lilting tune. Her first two stanzas contained these majestic words:

1. O Zion, haste, thy mission high fulfilling, To tell to all the
    world that God is Light;
    That He who made all nations is not willing, One soul
    should perish, lost in shades of night.
2. Behold how many thousands still are lying, Bound in the
    darkness prisonhouse of sin,
    With none to tell them of the Saviour's dying, Or of the
    life He died for them to win.

Eight years after this event took place, a forty-year old musician and composer in Bolton, Lancashire, England, James Walch, decided that since he was displeased with both

Henry Smart's tune "Pilgrims" and John Bacchus Dykes' tune "Angel's Song" for Faber's hymn "Hark, Hark My Soul", the only way he could resolve his conflict was to compose an original tune of his own for these familiar stanzas. This he then immediately proceeded to do, writing a third tune for Faber's poem, but leaving it for the time being unnamed. Although he may have questioned his ability to compose a piece of music that would eventually supplant either of the others in the esteem of the singing public, he little dreamed that, before the passing of many years, an editor would discover Mrs. Thomson's stanzas and his new tune, put them both together, and give Christendom the stirring strains of "O Zion, Haste", naming the music appropriately "Tidings". Although the composer died in 1901, seven years after "O Zion, Haste" appeared in the Episcopal "Church Hymnals" of 1894, the poet lived long enough to see the hymn growing in popularity and usefulness prior to her death, March 11, 1923, in her eighty-ninth year. Let us sing together several stanzas of this outstanding missionary hymn.

———————————

Two more Christian women were privileged to write acceptable missionary hymns and gospel songs, the hymn-writer being twenty-six year old Laura Scherer Copenhaver, who wrote "Heralds Of Christ" in 1894, being at that time a resident of Marion, Virginia, where her father, a prominent Lutheran clergyman, had founded Marion College. When she found herself unable to fill a scheduled speaking engagement at a Conference of Lutheran Church Women at Northfield, Massachusetts, that summer, she sent in her regrets, including in her letter the stanzas of the new missionary hymn as her "speech" for the assembled delegates. First sung at Northfield that summer to the thrilling tune "National Hymn" to which "God Of Our Fathers" is generally sung, her four stanzas were accorded a permanent place in ecumenical hymnody prior to the poet's death in 1940. Now copyrighted by the Woman's Missionary Society of The United Lutheran Church in America, Mrs. Copenhaver's hymn begins with this challenge:

Heralds of Christ, who bear the King's commands,
Immortal tidings in your mortal hands,
Pass on and carry swift the news ye bring;
Make straight, make straight the highway of the King.
Let us sing this stanza together, and, as we do, let us remember that the Christian religion alone of all the religions of the world has given to women the inspiration to write such magnificent hymns of praise, and has permitted their writings to stand alongside those of the men in the hearts and hymnals of our faith.

— — — — — — — —

The gospel song came from the pen of a minister's wife who lived all her fifty-six years in Fall River, Massachusetts, Mrs. Mary B. Slade (1826-1882) who, just nine years before her death, wrote the stanzas of the song that began:
From all the dark places of earth's heathen races,
O see how the thick shadows fly!
The voice of salvation awakes every nation,
"Come over and help us," they cry.
The Kingdom is coming, O tell ye the story, God's banner
        exalted shall be!
The earth shall be full of His knowledge and glory, As waters
        that cover the sea.
Set to a lilting tune by a southern gospel-song composer, R. M. McIntosh (1836-1899), this song gained great favor during the last quarter of the last century and the first quarter of the current century. Let us sing a stanza (or two) of Mrs. Slade's popular missionary gospel song.

— — — — — — — —

Strange as it seems, only one missionary ever succeeded in writing a successful missionary hymn, and he was Rev. Samuel Wolcott, who at the time of his unusual achievement was a fifty-six year old returned Congregational missionary attending a YMCA State Convention in Cleveland, Ohio, in 1869, after having spent some years as a representative of his church in Syria, both as a preacher and as a teacher. The slogan for that particular convention was "Christ For The

World And The World For Christ". Following one of the evening sessions, as a group of delegates visited informally outside the auditorium which served as convention headquarters, someone suggested that while the hymns being featured were all right, the convention would be enlivened as well as enriched if someone would write an original hymn around the theme or slogan for that year. Wolcott, a native of Connecticut, who was at that time the pastor of a Cleveland congregation, caught the inspiration of the moment, and, almost spontaneously wrote several stanzas in 6646664 poetic meter based upon the slogan, to be sung either to the tune "America" or "Italian Hymn, Trinity" (Come Thou Almighty King). His four stanzas all began with the same two phrases, although he developed each stanza differently:

Christ for the world we sing! The world to Christ we bring,
        With loving zeal;
The poor and them that mourn, The faint and overborne,
Sin-sick and sorrow-worn, Whom Christ doth heal.

While these lines are sometimes sung to the tune "Kirby Bedon" by Edward Bunnett, let us sing two stanzas to the tune "America" and two to "Italian Hymn, Trinity" since these tunes are much more familiar to our people.

Wolcott was so thrilled with the enthusiasm with which his first hymn was received, that, prior to his death in Massachusetts seventeen years later, in 1886, he wrote two-hundred more, none of which became as popular as his first.

— — — — — — — — —

Connecticut-born Doctor of Music Thomas Hastings (1784-1872) excelled as a composer, a poet and an editor, for he composed the beloved tune "Toplady" to which the hymn "Rock Of Ages" is universally sung; then as an editor, he was the man who took Simeon Marsh's music for Rev. John Newton's hymn, "Mary, To Her Saviour's Tomb" and set it to Charles Wesley's majestic hymn, "Jesus, Lover Of My Soul". As the tune "Martyn", it is now inextricably joined in hymnic marriage to Wesley, having been successfully divorced from Newton! Then, as a hymn-writer himself, he wrote the stanzas of a stirring missionary hymn in 1830, his co-worker and collaborator, Dr. Lowell Mason himself, composing the tune "Wesley";

Hail to the brightness of Zion's glad morning,
Joy to the lands that in darkness have lain!
Hushed be the accents of sorrow and mourning,
Zion in triumph begins her mild reign.

Let us sing the first stanza of this forceful hymn together, remembering that the poet was also an eminently successful composer and editor as well!

———————————

As for the rousing song, "We've A Story To Tell To The Nations", the words and music came from the talented pen of the British composer, Henry Ernest Nichol (1862-1928) in the year 1896, when he was thirty-four years of age. He considered his music better than his words, so he proudly signed his name as composer, but took the letters of Nichol, dropped the "h" and created a new name "Colin" and then followed that up by mixing up his second name "Ernest" until he came up with "Sterne" and wrote the name "Colin Sterne" as the author of the stanzas. Such modesty was unnecessary, however, since both words and music have found a permanent place in the hymnody of Christendom. Let us sing together the first stanza and Chorus of this hymn:

We've a story to tell to the nations, That will turn their
    hearts to the right,
A story of truth and mercy, A story of peace and light.
For the darkness shall turn to dawning, And the dawning to
    noonday bright,
And Christ's great kingdom shall come on earth, The king-
    dom of love and light.

———————————

Sir John Bowring (1792-1872) who was called "the worst governor-general in the history of Hong Kong", but who is remembered as the author of the hymn "In The Cross Of Christ I Glory", wrote the only question and answer missionary hymn, which was first published in the poet's own collection of "Hymns" in 1825. Taken from Isaiah 21:11-12,

"Watchman, what of the night? The morning cometh",
Bowring wrote these lines:
Watchman, tell us of the night, What its signs of promise
are.
Traveler, o'er yon mountain's height, See that glory-beaming
star!
Watchman, doth its beauteous ray, Aught of joy or hope
foretell?
Traveler, yes, it brings the day, Promised day of Israel.

Here a soloist and the congregation may sing these lines
antiphonally, or two people representing the Watchman and
the Traveler may sing the lines back and forth to each other,
dramatizing the message more effectively thereby, using the
familiar tune "Watchman", composed by Lowell Mason in
1830.

———————————

So our Missionary Hymns include Psalms, "Jesus Shall
Reign" (based upon Psalm 72); Hymns, "From Greenland's
Icy Mountains", and Spiritual Songs "From All The Dark
Places", and when we sing them we obey the admonition
of Paul found in Ephesians 5:18-19, "Be not drunk with
wine wherein is excess but be filled with the Spirit, speaking
to yourselves in psalms, hymns and spiritual songs, singing
and making melody in your heart to the Lord." Let us
rejoice that by means of these poems of praise we can voice
our own thanksgiving to God for His "unspeakable gift"
while keeping ever before us the demands of the Great Commission. Let us close our service by singing the first stanza
of: (Here the leader may suggest a stanza of "Jesus Saves",
words by Priscilla Owens and music by William J. Kirkpatrick, both in 1882; or Frances Havergal's gospel hymn "Tell
It Out Among The Nations That The Lord Is King" dated
April 19, 1872; or B. H. Draper's hymn "Ye Christian
Heralds, Go Proclaim", penned in 1803, to the tune "Missionary Chant" which H. C. Zeuner composed in 1832; or
any other appropriate and familiar missionary hymn or gospel song. Hymns and stanzas may be deleted or added according to the time available for this particular Hymn
Festival.)

MISCELLANEOUS
HYMN FESTIVAL PROGRAMS

MISCELLANEOUS
HYMN FESTIVAL PROGRAMS

An Alphabetical Hymn Festival

A Chronological Hymn Festival:
    HYMNS OF ALL CENTURIES

A Biblical Hymn Festival

A Geographical Hymn Festival:
    HYMNS OF ALL NATIONS

AN ALPHABETICAL HYMN FESTIVAL

Members of the congregation may be asked to suggest the hymns and songs for this service spontaneously during the program, provided no more than one selection is used for each letter of the alphabet. However, the program may also be prepared in advance, with congregational participation being broken up throughout the program by solos, duets or choral selections. Let only the first stanza of each song be used, so as not to make the service overly long and tiresome. For example, hymns and gospel songs may be used alphabetically in this manner:

All Hail The Power Of Jesus' Name
Blessed Assurance, Jesus Is Mine
Come Thou Almighty King
Does Jesus Care?
Eternal Father Strong To Save (The Navy Hymn)
Fairest Lord Jesus

God Of Grace And God Of Glory
Have Thine Own Way, Lord
I Need Thee Every Hour
Just As I Am Without One Plea
King Of The City Splendid (or Knocking, Knocking, Who Is There?)
Lead On, O King Eternal
More About Jesus Would I Know
Nearer My God To Thee
O Beautiful For Spacious Skies
Praise My Soul The King Of Heaven
Quiet From God! How Blessed Tis To Keep (or this letter may be omitted.)
Rock Of Ages
Sweet Hour Of Prayer
Take My Life And Let It Be
Under His Wings I Am Safely Abiding
Veni Sancte Spiritus (an ancient Latin Hymn translated: Come, Holy Ghost, In Love)
What A Friend We Have In Jesus
X: Except The Lord The Temple Build (or this letter may also be omitted)
Ye Servants Of God, Your Master Proclaim
Zion Stands By Hills Surrounded (also known as: Zion's King Shall Reign Victorious)

Appropriate substitutions may be made for any of these hymns and songs, since some will be familiar to one congregation and others to another. This is merely an idea that can be adapted to local situations, but is worth utilizing for a different kind of service of song and praise, around a specific theme, for the edification of the saints.

A CHRONOLOGICAL HYMN FESTIVAL

Hymns Of All Centuries

First Century: Read or Chant these passages from the New Testament which became the hymns of early Christians: Ave Maria of the angel Gabriel (Luke 1:26-35); The Magnificat of Mary (Luke 1:46-55); The Benedictus of Zechariah (Luke 1:68-79); The Gloria In Excelsis of the Angels (Luke 2:14); The Nunc Dimittis of Simeon (Luke 2:29-35).

Second Century: The Gloria Patri (to any of a number of familiar tunes).

Third Century: Shepherd of Tender Youth; by Clement of Alexandria; translated into English poetic form by Rev. Henry Dexter.

Fourth Century: Te Deum Laudamus (Any of the many translations of "We Praise Thee, O God"); O Splendor Of God's Glory Bright, by Ambrose of Milan (340-397).

Fifth Century: Of The Father's Love Begotten, by Aurelius Clements Prudentius (348-413).

Sixth Century: Welcome, Happy Morning, by Venantius Fortunatus (530-609), translated by Rev. John Ellerton.

Seventh Century: Christian, Dost Thou See Them? by Andrew of Crete (660-732), translated by Rev. John Neale.

Eighth Century: The Day Of Resurrection, by John of Damascus; translated by Neale.

Ninth Century: All Glory, Laud And Honor, by Theodulph of Orleans; translated by Neale.

Tenth Century: Father We Praise Thee, Now The Night Is Over; Anonymous; translated by Percy Dreamer.

Eleventh Century: O Quanta Qualia, by Peter Abelard (1079-1142); translated by Neale into the hymn O What Their Joy And Their Glory Must Be.

Twelfth Century: O Sacred Head Now Wounded, by Bernard of Clairvaux, translated into German and from the German into English by Rev. James W. Alexander.

Thirteenth Century: All Creatures Of Our God And King, by St. Francis of Assisi.

Fourteenth Century: The God Of Abraham Praise, by Daniel ben Judah.

Fifteenth Century: O Sons And Daughters Let Us Sing, by Jean Tisserand, 1494.

Sixteenth Century: A Mighty Fortress Is Our God; words and music by Martin Luther.

Seventeenth Century: The Doxology by Bishop Thomas Ken.

Eighteenth Century: Joy To The World, by Isaac Watts; Jesus, Lover Of My Soul, by Charles Wesley; All Hail The Power Of Jesus' Name, by Edward Peronnet.

Nineteenth Century: America, by Samuel Francis Smith; Onward Christian Soldiers by Sabine Baring-Gould; Holy, Holy, Holy, by Reginald Heber.

Twentieth Century: I Would Be True, by Howard A. Walter; Rise Up O Men Of God, by William Pierson Merrill; God Of Grace And God Of Glory, by Harry Emerson Fosdick.

Any other appropriate or familiar hymns, sacred solos, instrumental or choral selections may be substituted for any of those mentioned for the various centuries, as long as the main purpose for the Hymn Festival is recognized, that purpose being to demonstrate how God has continuously raised up people in every age and from every generation to sing His praises. He did not stop singing when David died nor did He stop singing when Wesley died. He is always singing and will continue so to do as long as man responds to His love and opens His heart to receive Him.

A BIBLICAL HYMN FESTIVAL

Many of the larger Hymnals contain an INDEX OF SCRIPTURAL TEXTS or an INDEX OF SCRIPTURAL ALLUSIONS, listing the many chapters and verses from the books of the Bible, and the hymns or the stanzas of different hymns based upon, inspired by or suggestive of those passages of Scripture. By selecting one such hymn or stanza from many of the thirty-nine books of the Old Testament, an evening could be well spent if the leader read the passage and then asked the congregation to join in singing the stanza or hymn. Thus, one could have both AN OLD TESTAMENT HYMN FESTIVAL, and, by doing the same thing for the twenty-seven books of the New Testament, could have A NEW TESTAMENT HYMN FESTIVAL. However, by selecting familiar hymns and gospel songs and then checking back through this Index, one could prepare an interesting program for A BIBLICAL HYMN FESTIVAL, choosing only those hymns and songs with which the congregation is familiar, and just enough of them to fill the allotted time. This type of service would have a two-fold function, being both instructive and inspirational.

A GEOGRAPHICAL HYMN FESTIVAL

Hymns Of All Nations

Germany: When Morning Gilds The Skies, translated by the British clergyman Rev. Edward Caswell in 1853 from an anonymous German hymn of the year 1800. We Plow The Fields And Scatter; by Matthias Claudius, 1782; translated into English by Miss Jane Campbell in 1861.

Austria: Silent Night, Holy Night; by Father Joseph Mohr and Organist Franz Gruber, Christmas Eve, 1818.

Egypt: Shepherd Of Tender Youth, by Clement of Alexandria, in the second century; translated into English by Rev. Henry Dexter in 1846. This is the earliest hymn in existence outside of the New Testament hymns which early Christians sang during the first centuries of the Christian era.

Italy: Welcome Happy Morning, by the sixth-century Italian troubadour, Venantius Fortunatus; translated into English by Rev. John Ellerton in 1869. All Creatures Of Our God And King, by St. Francis of Assisi, the thirteenth-century spiritual leader; translated into English by Rev. William Henry Draper in 1926.

Palestine: Art Thou Weary, Art Thou Languid (Troubled)? by St. Stephen the Sabaite in the eighth century; translated by Rev. John Mason Neale in 1868.

Japan: Let There Be Light, Lord God Of Hosts, written by Rev. William M. Vories near Lake Bewa, Japan, in 1908.

Scotland: O Love That Wilt Not Let Me Go, by the distinguished blind clergyman Rev. George Matheson at his manse at Innellan, Argylshire in 1882. Beneath The Cross Of Jesus, by Miss Elizabeth Cecelia Clephane in 1872. (She also wrote The Ninety And Nine, which could be used as a solo here.)

Ireland: Jesus Calls Us, by Mrs. Cecil Frances Alexander in 1852, while her husband was serving as Primate of the Anglican Church for all of Ireland.

Wales: Once To Every Man And Nation, or any other hymn that fits the stirring tune Ton-Y-Botel, the Welsh hymntune that means "Tune that came out of a bottle", composed by the Welshman, Thomas John Williams, in 1890. (This tune is also known in some places as "Ebenezer".)

England: Joy To The World, by Rev. Isaac Watts, 1719; or Holy, Holy, Holy, by Rev. Reginald Heber, 1826; or Jesus Lover Of My Soul, by Rev. Charles Wesley, 1740.

Canada: What A Friend We Have In Jesus, by Joseph Scriven about 1855.

The United States: Rise Up O Men Of God, by Rev. William Pierson Merrill in 1911; or Blessed Assurance, by Fanny Crosby, 1873.

France: O Holy Night (Cantique de Noel) by the French composer, Adolph Adam (as a solo).

Poland: Infant Holy, Infant Lowly, the Christmas carol translated from a Polish poem "In Manger Lying" by Miss Edith Redd about 1925.

The Scandinavian countries: The tune "Tempus Adest Floridum" to which either "Good King Wenceslaus" or "Gentle Mary Laid Her Child" is sung; probably composed by Theodoricus Petrus of Nyland, Finland about 1582; printed in a Finland-Sweden Lutheran collection, discovered at Stockholm and sent to the British clergyman Dr. John Mason Neale, who arranged his carol "Good King Wenceslaus" to match its meter.

Switzerland: I Greet Thee, Who My Sure Redeemer Art, by Rev. John Calvin in 1545, during his stay in Geneva, Switzerland.

Russia: Now On Land And Sea Descending, by Rev. Samuel Longfellow, 1859; set to the tune "Vesper Hymn" which the Russian musician Dimitri S. Bortniansky composed in 1818. God The Omnipotent! by Henry Chorley, 1842; set to the thrilling music of a Russian national anthem composed by Alexis Lwoff in 1833, and entitled now "Russian Hymn".

China: O Bread Of Life, For All Men Broken, by Timothy T'ingfang Lew, 1936; translated by Rev. Frank Price in 1952.

Greece: The melody of Jemima Luke's children's hymn, I Think When I Read That Sweet Story Of Old, 1841; arranged for this hymn by William Bradbury in 1859.

India: The music for the Scots poet's gospel song, There Is A Happy Land, written by Andrew Young to match a tune from India known simply as "Happy Land", in 1838.